'As skilled in writing as he is in medicine, [his] inclination
is to look beyond the disability at hand to see what it
can teach us about the human condition . . . Sacks's
enthusiasm for signs is contagious'
Peter S. Prescott, *Newsweek*

'Oliver Sacks, so widely recognised as a successful neurologist
and writer, is well-placed to play the Ancient Mariner and
hold us with his latest thought-provoking tale: deafness
in children, a more familiar topic for the layman than the
nervous disorders he has written about previously . . . Sacks
manages to convey his own sympathetic review of the deaf as
an attractive, self-reliant minority, with a highly developed
sensibility and a vivid language all their own'
The Times

'Sacks's latest work, however, sees him reaching almost a
demedicalisation standpoint, by treating the world of the deaf
from a cultural or ethnic perspective . . . Sacks takes his reader
on a three-part journey into the world of the deaf'
Eoin Devereux, *Sunday Tribune*

'*Seeing Voices* charts the often outrageous ways the deaf have
been treated and their continuing struggle for acceptance
in the hearing world'
Danae Brook, *Sunday Express*

'Dr Sacks's main virtue is that he makes you want to switch roles
all the time . . . Dr Sacks, whose heart is in the right place, wants
the deaf to have all they need, but most of all their own natural
and private language. He brings afresh to our attention
a problem that is never going to be easily solved'
Paul West, *New York Times Book Review*

SEEING VOICES

OLIVER SACKS is a physician and the author of many books, including *The Man Who Mistook His Wife for a Hat*, *Awakenings* (which inspired the Oscar-nominated film) and *Musicophilia*. Born in London and educated at Oxford, he now lives in New York City, where he is Professor of Neurology and Psychiatry at Columbia University. He is the first, and only, Columbia University Artist, and is also a Fellow of the Royal College of Physicians. In 2008, he was appointed Commander of the British Empire.

For more information, visit
www.oliversacks.com

SEEING VOICES

A JOURNEY INTO THE WORLD OF THE DEAF

OLIVER SACKS

PICADOR

First published 1989 by the University of California Press, Berkeley and Los Angeles

First published in paperback 1990 by Harper Perennial, New York

First published in Great Britain 1990 by Picador

New edition first published 2000 by Vintage Books, a division of Random House Inc., New York
and simultaneously in Canada by Random House of Canada Limited, Toronto

New edition first published in Great Britain 2009 by Picador

This edition published 2012 by Picador
an imprint of Pan Macmillan,
20 New Wharf Road, London N1 9RR

Associated companies throughout the world
www.panmacmillan.com

ISBN 978-0-330-52364-6

The author gratefully acknowledges permission to reprint material from
Language and the Discovery of Reality by Joseph Church, reprinted by permission of the author;
Death in America by Carol Padden and John Humphries, reprinted by permission of Harvard University Press;
and *Deafness*, copyright 1969 by David Wright, reprinted by permission of Stein and Day Publishers.

5 7 9 8 6

A CIP catalogue record for this book is available from
the British Library.

Printed and bound by CPI Group (UK) Ltd, Croydon, CR0 4YY

Visit **www.picador.com** to read more about all our books
and to buy them. You will also find features, author interviews and
news of any author events, and you can sign up for e-newsletters
so that you're always first to hear about our new releases.

For

Isabelle Rapin,

Bob Johnson,

Bob Silvers,

and Kate Edgar

[Sign language] is, in the hands of its masters, a most beautiful and expressive language, for which, in their intercourse with each other and as a means of easily and quickly reaching the minds of the deaf, neither nature nor art has given them a satisfactory substitute.

It is impossible for those who do not understand it to comprehend its possibilities with the deaf, its powerful influence on the moral and social happiness of those deprived of hearing, and its wonderful power of carrying thought to intellects which would otherwise be in perpetual darkness. Nor can they appreciate the hold it has upon the deaf. So long as there are two deaf people upon the face of the earth and they get together, so long will signs be in use.

—J. Schuyler Long
Head teacher, Iowa School for the Deaf
The Sign Language (1910)

CONTENTS

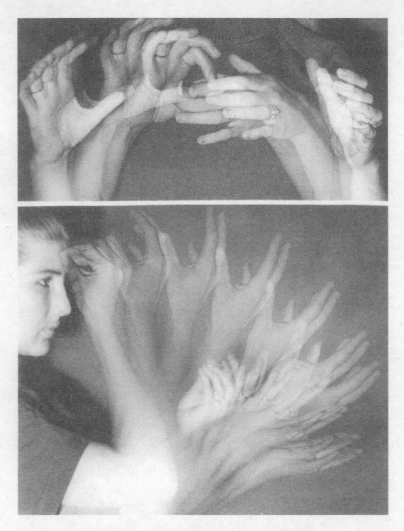

Strobe photograph of ASL signs "join" and "inform."

(Reprinted by permission from *The Signs of Language*,
E. S. Klima & U. Bellugi. Harvard University Press, 1979.)

PREFACE

THREE years ago I knew nothing of the situation of the deaf, and never imagined that it could cast light on so many realms, above all, on the realm of language. I was astonished to learn about the history of deaf people, and the extraordinary (linguistic) challenges they face, astonished too to learn of a completely visual language, Sign, a language different in mode from my own language, Speech.[1] It is all too easy to take language, one's own language, for granted—one may need to encounter another language, or rather another *mode* of language, in order to be astonished, to be pushed into wonder, again.

When I first read of the deaf and their singular mode of language, Sign, I was incited to embark on an exploration, a journey. This journey took me to deaf people and their families; to schools for the deaf, and to Gallaudet, the unique university of the deaf; it took me to Martha's Vineyard, where there used to exist a hereditary deafness and where everybody (hearing no less than deaf) spoke Sign; it took me to towns like Fremont and Rochester, where there is a remarkable interface of deaf and hearing communities; it took me to the great researchers on Sign, and the conditions of the deaf—brilliant and dedicated researchers who communicated to me their excitement, their sense of unexplored regions and new frontiers. My journey has taken me to look at language, at the nature of talking and teaching, at child development, at the development and functioning of the nervous system, at the formation of communities, worlds, and cultures, in a way which was wholly new to me, and which has been an education and a delight. It has, above all, afforded a completely new perspective on age-old problems, a new and unexpected view onto language, biology, and culture . . . it has made the familiar strange, and the strange familiar.

My travels left me both enthralled and appalled. I was appalled as I discovered how many of the deaf never acquire the powers of good language—or thinking—and how poor a life might lie in store for them.

But almost at once I was to be made aware of another dimension, another world of considerations, not biological, but cultural. Many of the deaf people I met had not merely acquired good language, but language of an entirely different sort, a language that served not only the powers of thought (and indeed allowed thought and perception of a kind not wholly imaginable by the hearing), but served as the medium of a rich community and culture. Whilst I never forgot the "medical" status of the deaf, I had now to see them in a new, "ethnic" light, as a people, with a distinctive language, sensibility, and culture of their own.[2]

It might be thought that the story and study of deaf people, and their language, is something of extremely limited interest. But this, I believe, is by no means the case. It is true that the congenitally deaf only constitute about 0.1 percent of the population, but the considerations that arise from them raise issues of the widest and deepest importance. The study of the deaf shows us that much of what is distinctively human in us—our capacities for language, for thought, for communication, and culture—do not develop automatically in us, are not just biological functions, but are, equally, social and historical in origin; that they are a *gift*—the most wonderful of gifts—from one generation to another. We see that Culture is as crucial as Nature.

The existence of a visual language, Sign, and of the striking enhancements of perception and visual intelligence that go with its acquisition, shows us that the brain is rich in potentials we would scarcely have guessed of, shows us the almost unlimited plasticity and resource of the nervous system, the human organism, when it is faced with the new and must adapt. If this subject shows us the vulnerabilities, the ways in which (often unwittingly) we may harm ourselves, it shows us, equally, our unknown and unexpected strengths, the infinite resources for survival and transcendence which Nature and Culture, together, have given us. Thus, although I hope that deaf people, and their families, teachers, and friends, may find this book of special interest, I hope that the general reader may turn to it, too, for an unexpected perspective on the human condition.

THIS book is in three parts. The first, "A Deaf World," was written in 1985 and 1986, and started as a review of a book on the history of the deaf, Harlan Lane's *When the Mind Hears.* This had expanded to an essay by the time it was published (in the *New York Review of Books*, March 27, 1986), and has since been further enlarged and revised. I have, however, left certain formulations and locutions, with which I no longer fully agree, in place, because I felt I should preserve the original, whatever its defects, as reflecting the way I first thought about the subject. Part III, "The Revolution of the Deaf," was stimulated by the revolt of the students at Gallaudet in March 1988, and was published in the *New York Review of Books* on June 2, 1988. This too has been considerably revised and enlarged for the present book. Part II, "Thinking in Sign," was written last, in the fall of 1988, but is, in some ways, the heart of the book—at least the most systematic, but also the most personal, view of the whole subject. I should add that I have never found it possible to tell a story, or pursue a line of thought, without taking innumerable side trips or excursions along the way, and finding my journey the richer for this.[3]

I am, I should emphasize, an outsider in this field—I am not deaf, I do not sign, I am not an interpreter or teacher, I am not an expert on child development, and I am neither a historian nor a linguist. This is, as will be apparent, a charged (at times embattled) area, where passionate opinions have contended for centuries. I am an outsider, with no special knowledge or expertise, but also, I think, with no prejudices, no ax to grind, no animus in the matter.

I could not have made my journey, let alone written about it, without the aid and inspiration of innumerable others: first and foremost deaf people—patients, subjects, collaborators, friends—the only people who can give one an inside perspective; and those most directly concerned with them, their families, interpreters, and teachers. In particular I must acknowledge here the great help of Sarah Elizabeth and Sam Lewis, and their daughter Charlotte; Deborah Tannen of Georgetown University; and the staffs at the California School for the Deaf at Fremont, the Lexington School for the Deaf, and many other schools and institutions for the deaf, most especially Gallaudet University—including David de Lorenzo, Carol Erting, Michael Karchmer, Scott Liddell, Jane Norman,

John Van Cleve, Bruce White, and James Woodward, among many others.

I owe a central debt to those researchers who have made it their lifelong concern to understand and study the deaf and their language—in particular, Ursula Bellugi, Susan Schaller, Hilde Schlesinger, and William Stokoe, who have shared their thoughts and observations fully and generously with me, and stimulated my own. Jerome Bruner, who has thought so profoundly about the mental and language development of children, has been an invaluable friend and guide throughout. My friend and colleague Elkhonon Goldberg has suggested new ways of considering the neurological foundations of language and thought, and the special forms this may take in the deaf. I have had the special pleasure, this year, of meeting Harlan Lane and Nora Ellen Groce, whose books so inspired me in 1986, at the start of my journey, and Carol Padden, whose book so influenced me in 1988—their perspectives on the deaf have enlarged my own thought. Several colleagues, including Ursula Bellugi, Jerome Bruner, Robert Johnson, Harlan Lane, Helen Neville, Isabelle Rapin, Israel Rosenfield, Hilde Schlesinger, and William Stokoe, have read the manuscript of this book at various stages and offered comments, criticism, and support, for which I am particularly grateful. To all these and many others, I owe illumination and insights (though my opinions—and mistakes—are wholly my own).

In March of 1986, Stan Holwitz of the University of California Press instantly responded to my first essay, and urged and encouraged me to expand it into a book; he has given patient support and stimulus during the three years it has taken to realize his suggestion. Paula Cizmar read successive drafts of the book, and offered me many valuable suggestions. Shirley Warren has guided the manuscript through production, dealing patiently with ever more footnotes and last-minute changes.

I am much indebted to my niece, Elizabeth Sacks Chase, who suggested the title—it derives from Pyramus's words to Thisbe: "I see a voice. . . ."

Since completing this book, I have started to do what, perhaps, I should have done at the start—I have begun to learn Sign. I owe special thanks to my teacher, Janice Rimler, of the New York Society for the Deaf, and to my tutors, Amy and Mark Trugman, for struggling valiantly with a difficult, late beginner—and convincing me that it is never too late to begin.

Finally I must acknowledge the deepest debt of all to four people—two colleagues and two editors—who have played a central part in making possible my work and writing. First to Bob Silvers, editor of the *New York Review of Books*, who sent me Harlan Lane's book in the first place, saying, "You've never really thought about language; this book will force you to"—as indeed it did. Bob Silvers has a clairvoyant sense of what people have not yet thought about, but should; and, with his special obstetric gift, helps to deliver them of their as-yet-unborn thoughts.

Second, to Isabelle Rapin, who has been my closest friend and colleague at the Albert Einstein College of Medicine for twenty years, and who herself has worked with the deaf, and thought deeply about them, for a quarter of a century. Isabelle introduced me to deaf patients, took me to schools for the deaf, shared with me her experience of deaf children, and helped me understand the problems of the deaf as I could never have done unaided. (She herself wrote an extensive essay-review [Rapin, 1986] based chiefly on *When the Mind Hears*.)

I first met Bob Johnson, chairman of the linguistics department at Gallaudet, on my first visit there in 1986, and was introduced by him both to Sign, and to the world of the deaf—a language, a culture, that outsiders can scarcely enter or imagine. If Isabelle Rapin, with Bob Silvers, launched me on this journey, Bob Johnson then took over as my traveling companion and guide.

Kate Edgar, finally, has filled a unique role as collaborator, friend, editor, and organizer, inciting me at all times to think and write, to see the full aspectuality of the subject, but always to hold on to its focus and center.

To these four people, then, I dedicate this book.

O. W. S.

New York
March 1989

SEEING VOICES

A Deaf World

WE are remarkably ignorant about deafness, which Dr. Johnson called "one of the most desperate of human calamities"—much more ignorant than an educated man would have been in 1886, or 1786. Ignorant and indifferent. During the last few months I have raised the subject with countless people and nearly always met with responses like: "Deafness? Don't know any deaf people. Never thought much about it. There's nothing *interesting* about deafness, is there?" This would have been my own response a few months ago.

Things changed for me when I was sent a fat book by Harlan Lane called *When the Mind Hears: A History of the Deaf*, which I opened with indifference, soon to be changed to astonishment, and then to something approaching incredulity. I discussed the subject with my friend and colleague Dr. Isabelle Rapin, who has worked closely with the deaf for twenty-five years. I got to know better a congenitally deaf colleague, a remarkable and highly gifted woman, whom I had previously taken for granted.[1] I started seeing, or exploring for the first time, a number of deaf patients under my care.[2] My reading rapidly spread from Harlan Lane's history to *The Deaf Experience*, a collection of memoirs by and about the first literate deaf, edited by Lane, and then to Nora Ellen Groce's *Everyone Here Spoke Sign Language*, and to a great many other books. Now I have an entire bookshelf on a subject that I had not thought of even as existing six months ago, and have seen some of the remarkable films that have been produced on the subject.[3]

One more acknowledgment by way of preamble. In 1969 W. H. Auden gave me a copy, his own copy, of *Deafness*, a remarkable autobiographical memoir by the South African poet and novelist David Wright, who became deaf at the age of seven. "You'll find it fascinating," he said. "It's a wonderful book." It was dotted with his own annotations (though I do not know whether he ever reviewed it). I skimmed it, without paying more attention, in 1969. But now I was to rediscover it for myself. David Wright is a writer who writes from the depths of his own experience—and not as a historian or scholar writes about a subject. Moreover, he is not alien to us. We can easily imagine, more or less, what it would be like to be him (whereas we cannot without difficulty imagine what it would be like to be someone born deaf, like the famous deaf teacher Laurent Clerc). Thus he can serve as a bridge for us, conveying us through his own experiences into the realm of the unimaginable. Since Wright is easier to read than the great mutes of the eighteenth century, he should if possible be read first—for he prepares us for them. Toward the close of the book he writes:

Not much as been written about deafness by the deaf.[4] Even so, considering that I did not become deaf till *after* I had learned the language, I am no better placed than a hearing person to imagine what it is like to be born into silence and reach the age of reason without acquiring a vehicle for thought and communication. Merely to try gives weight to the tremendous opening of St. John's Gospel: In the beginning was the Word. How does one formulate concepts in such a condition?

It is this—the relation of language to thought—that forms the deepest, the ultimate issue when we consider what faces or may face those who are born, or very early become, deaf.

The term "deaf" is vague, or rather, is so general that it impedes consideration of the vastly differing degrees of deafness, degrees that are of qualitative, and even of "existential," significance. There are the "hard of hearing," fifteen million or so in the U.S. population, who can manage to hear some speech using hearing aids and a certain amount of care and patience on the part of those who speak to them. Many of us have parents or grandparents in this category—a century ago they would have used ear trumpets; now they use hearing aids.

There are also the "severely deaf," many as a result of ear disease or injury in early life; but with them, as with the hard of hearing, the hearing of speech is still possible, especially with the new, highly sophisticated, computerized, and "personalized" hearing aids now becoming available. Then there are the "profoundly deaf"—sometimes called "stone deaf"—who have no hope at all of hearing any speech, whatever imaginable technological advances are made. Profoundly deaf people cannot converse in the usual way—they must either lip-read (as David Wright did), or use sign language, or both.

It is not merely the degree of deafness that matters but—crucially—the age, or stage, at which it occurs. David Wright, in the passage already quoted, observes that he lost his hearing only after he had acquired language, and (this being the case) he cannot even imagine what it must be like for those who lack or have lost hearing before the acquisition of language. He brings this out in other passages.

> My becoming deaf when I did—if deafness had to be my destiny—was remarkably lucky. By the age of seven a child will have grasped the essentials of language, as I had. Having learned naturally how to speak was another advantage—pronunciation, syntax, inflexion, idiom, all had come by ear. I had the basis of a vocabulary which could easily be extended by reading. *All of these would have been denied me had I been born deaf or lost my hearing earlier than I did.* [Italics added.]

Wright speaks of the "phantasmal voices" that he hears when anyone speaks to him provided he can *see* the movement of their lips and faces, and of how he would "hear" the soughing of the wind whenever he saw trees or branches being stirred by the wind.[5] He gives a fascinating description of this first happening—of its *immediate* occurrence with the onset of deafness:

> [My deafness] was made more difficult to perceive because from the very first my eyes had unconsciously begun to translate motion into sound. My mother spent most of the day beside me and I understood everything she said. Why not? Without knowing it I had been reading her mouth all my life. When she spoke I seemed to hear her voice. It was an illusion which persisted even after I knew it was an illusion. My father, my cousin, everyone I had known, retained phantasmal voices. That they were imaginary, the projections of habit and memory, did not come home to me until I had left the hospital. One day I was talking with my cousin and he, in a moment of

inspiration, covered his mouth with his hand as he spoke. Silence! Once and for all I understood that when I could not see I could not hear.[6]

Though Wright knows the sounds he "hears" to be "illusory"— "projections of habit and memory"—they remain intensely vivid for him throughout the decades of his deafness. For Wright, for those deafened after hearing is well established, the world may remain full of sounds even though they are "phantasmal."[7]

It is another matter entirely, and one that is essentially unimaginable, by the normal (and even by the postlingually deafened, like David Wright), if hearing is absent at birth, or lost in infancy before the language is acquired. Those so afflicted— the prelingually deaf—are in a category qualitatively different from all others. For these people, who have never heard, who have no possible auditory memories, images, or associations, there can never be even the illusion of sound. They live in a world of utter, unbroken soundlessness and silence.[8] These, the congenitally deaf, number perhaps a quarter of a million in this country. They make up a thousandth of the world's children.

It is with these and these only that we will be concerned here, for their situation and predicament are unique. Why should this be so? People tend, if they think of deafness at all, to think of it as less grave than blindness, to see it as a disadvantage, or a nuisance, or a handicap, but scarcely as devastating in a radical sense.

Whether deafness is "preferable" to blindness, if acquired in later life, is arguable; but to be born deaf is infinitely more serious than to be born blind—at least potentially so. For the prelingually deaf, unable to hear their parents, risk being severely retarded, if not permanently defective, in their grasp of language unless early and effective measures are taken. And to be defective in language, for a human being, is one of the most desperate of calamities, for it is only through language that we enter fully into our human estate and culture, communicate freely with our fellows, acquire and share information. If we cannot do this, we will be bizarrely disabled and cut off—whatever our desires, or endeavors, or native capacities. And indeed, we may be so little able to realize our intellectual capacities as to appear mentally defective.[9]

It was for this reason that the congenitally deaf, or "deaf and dumb," were considered "dumb" (stupid) for thousands of years and were regarded by an unenlightened law as "incompetent"— to inherit property, to marry, to receive education, to have adequately challenging work—and were denied fundamental human rights. This situation did not begin to be remedied until the middle of the eighteenth century, when (perhaps as part of a more general enlightenment, perhaps as a specific act of empathy and genius) the perception and situation of the deaf were radically altered.

The *philosophes* of the time were clearly fascinated by the extraordinary issues and problems posed by a seemingly languageless human being. Indeed, the Wild Boy of Aveyron,[10] when brought to Paris in 1800, was admitted to the National Institution for Deaf-Mutes, which was at the time supervised by the Abbé Roch-Ambroise Sicard, a founding member of the Society of Observers of Man, and a notable authority on the education of the deaf. As Jonathan Miller writes:[11]

As far as the members of this society were concerned the "savage" child represented an ideal case with which to investi-

gate the foundations of human nature. . . . By studying a creature of this sort, just as they had previously studied savages
and primitives, Red Indians and orangutans, the intellectuals
of the late eighteenth century hoped to decide what was characteristic of Man. Perhaps it would now be possible to weigh
the native endowment of the human species and to settle once
and for all the part that was played by society in the development of language, intelligence, and morality.

Here, of course, the two enterprises diverged, one ending in
triumph, the other in complete failure. The Wild Boy never
acquired language, for whatever reason or reasons. One insufficiently considered possibility is that he was, strangely, never
exposed to sign language, but continually (and vainly) forced to
try to speak. But when the "deaf and dumb" were properly
approached, i.e., through sign language, they proved eminently
educable, and they rapidly showed an astonished world how
fully they could enter into its culture and life. This wonderful
circumstance—how a despised or neglected minority, practically denied human status up to this point, emerged suddenly
and startlingly upon the world stage (and the later tragic
undermining of all this in the following century)—constitutes
the opening chapter of the history of the deaf.

But let us, before launching on this strange history, go back
to the wholly personal and "innocent" observations of David
Wright ("innocent" because, as he himself stresses, he made a
point of avoiding any reading on the subject until he had written his own book). At the age of eight, when it became clear that
his deafness was incurable, and that without special measures
his speech would regress, he was sent to a special school in

England, one of the ruthlessly dedicated, but misconceived, rigorously "oral" schools, which are concerned above all to make the deaf speak like other children, and which have done so much harm to the prelingually deaf since their inception. The young David Wright was flabbergasted at his first encounter with the prelingually deaf.

Sometimes I took lessons with Vanessa. She was the first deaf child I had met. . . . But even to an eight-year-old like myself her general knowledge seemed strangely limited. I remember a geography lesson we were doing together, when Miss Neville asked,

"Who is the king of England?"

Vanessa didn't know; troubled, she tried to read sideways the geography book, which lay open at the chapter about Great Britain that we had prepared.

"King—king," began Vanessa.

"Go on," commanded Miss Neville.

"I know," I said.

"Be quiet."

"United Kingdom," said Vanessa.

I laughed.

"You are very silly," said Miss Neville. "How can a king be called 'United Kingdom'?"

"King United Kingdom," tried poor Vanessa, scarlet.

"Tell her if you know, [David]."

"King George the Fifth," I said proudly.

"It's not fair! It wasn't in the book!"

Vanessa was quite right of course; the chapter on the geography of Great Britain did not concern itself with its political setup. She was far from stupid; but having been born deaf her slowly and painfully acquired vocabulary was still too small to allow her to read for amusement or pleasure. As a consequence there were almost no means by which she could pick up the fund of miscellaneous and temporarily useless information other children unconsciously acquire from conversation or random reading. Almost everything she knew she had been taught or made to learn. And this is a fundamental difference between hearing and deaf-born children—or was, in that pre-electronic era.

Vanessa's situation, one sees, was a serious one, despite her native ability; and it was helped only with much difficulty, if not actually perpetuated, by the sort of teaching and communication forced upon her. For in this progressive school, as it was regarded, there was an almost insanely fierce, righteous prohibition of sign language—not only of the standard British Sign Language but of the "sign-argot"—the rough sign language developed on their own by the deaf children in the school. And yet—this is also well described by Wright—signing flourished at the school, was irrepressible despite punishment and prohibition. This was young David Wright's first vision of the boys:

Confusion stuns the eye, arms whirl like windmills in a hurricane ... the emphatic silent vocabulary of the body—look, expression, bearing, glance of eye; hands perform their pantomime. Absolutely engrossing pandemonium. . . . I begin to sort out what's going on. The seemingly corybantic brandishing of hands and arms reduces itself to a convention, a code which as yet conveys nothing. It is in fact a kind of vernacular. The school has evolved its own peculiar language or argot, though not a verbal one. . . . All communications were sup-

posed to be oral. Our own sign-argot was of course prohibited. . . . But these rules could not be enforced without the
presence of the staff. What I have been describing is not how
we talked, but how we talked among ourselves when no hearing person was present. At such times our behaviour and conversation were quite different. We relaxed inhibitions, wore
no masks.

Such was the Northampton School in the English Midlands,
when David Wright went there as a pupil in 1927. For him, as a
postlingually deaf child, with a firm grasp of language, the
school was, manifestly, excellent. For Vanessa, for other prelingually deaf children, such a school, with its ruthlessly oral
approach, was not short of a disaster. But a century earlier, say,
in the American Asylum for the Deaf, opened a decade before in
Hartford, Connecticut, where there was free use of sign language between all pupils and teachers, Vanessa would not have
found herself pitifully handicapped; she might have become a
literate, perhaps even literary, young woman of the sort who
emerged and wrote books during the 1830s.

The situation of the prelingually deaf, prior to 1750, was indeed
a calamity: unable to acquire speech, hence "dumb" or "mute";
unable to enjoy free communication with even their parents and
families; confined to a few rudimentary signs and gestures; cut
off, except in large cities, even from the community of their own
kind; deprived of literacy and education, all knowledge of the
world; forced to do the most menial work; living alone, often
close to destitution; treated by the law and society as little better
than imbeciles—the lot of the deaf was manifestly dreadful.[12]

But what was manifest was as nothing to the destitution inside—the destitution of knowledge and thought that prelingual deafness could bring, in the absence of any communication or remedial measures. The deplorable state of the deaf aroused both the curiosity and the compassion of the *philosophes*. Thus the Abbé Sicard asked:

> *Why* is the uneducated deaf person isolated in nature and unable to communicate with other men? *Why* is he reduced to this state of imbecility? Does his biological constitution differ from ours? Does he not have everything he needs for having sensations, acquiring ideas, and combining them to do everything that we do? Does he not get sensory impressions from objects as we do? Are these not, as with us, the occasion of the mind's sensations and its acquired ideas? *Why* then does the deaf person remain stupid while we become intelligent?

To ask this question—never really or clearly asked before—is to grasp its answer, to see that the answer lies in the use of symbols. It is, Sicard continues, because the deaf person has "no symbols for fixing and combining ideas . . . that there is a total communication-gap between him and other people." But what was all-important, and had been a source of fundamental confusion since Aristotle's pronouncements on the matter, was the enduring misconception that symbols had to be speech. Perhaps indeed this passionate misperception, or prejudice, went back to biblical days: the subhuman status of mutes was part of the Mosaic code, and it was reinforced by the biblical exaltation of the voice and ear as the one and true way in which man and God could speak ("In the beginning was the Word"). And yet, overborne by Mosaic and Aristotelian thunderings, some profound voices intimated that this need not be so. Thus Socrates' remark in the *Cratylus* of Plato, which so impressed the youthful Abbé de l'Epée:

> If we had neither voice nor tongue, and yet wished to manifest things to one another, should we not, like those which are at present mute, endeavour to signify our meaning by the hands, head, and other parts of the body?

Or the deep, yet obvious, insights of the physician-philosopher Cardan in the sixteenth century:

> It is possible to place a deaf-mute in a position to hear by reading, and to speak by writing . . . for as different sounds are conventionally used to signify different things, so also may the various figures of objects and words. . . . Written characters and ideas may be connected without the intervention of actual sounds.

In the sixteenth century the notion that the understanding of ideas did not depend upon the hearing of words was revolutionary.[13]

But it is not (usually) the ideas of philosophers that change reality; nor, conversely, is it the practice of ordinary people. What changes history, what kindles revolutions, is the meeting of the two. A lofty mind—that of the Abbé de l'Epée—had to meet a humble usage—the indigenous sign language of the poor deaf who roamed Paris—in order to make possible a momentous transformation. If we ask why this meeting had not occurred before, it has something to do with the vocation of the

Abbé, who could not bear to think of the souls of the deaf-mute living and dying unshriven, deprived of the Catechism, the Scriptures, the Word of God; and it is partly owing to his humility—that he *listened* to the deaf—and partly to a philosophical and linguistic idea then very much in the air—that of universal language, like the *speceium* of which Leibniz dreamed.[14] Thus, de l'Epée approached sign language not with contempt but with awe.

> The universal language that your scholars have sought for in vain and of which they have despaired, is here; it is right before your eyes, it is the mimicry of the impoverished deaf. Because you do not know it, you hold it in contempt, yet it alone will provide you with the key to all languages.

That this was a misapprehension—for sign language is not a universal language in this grand sense, and Leibniz's noble dream was probably a chimera—did not matter, was even an advantage.[15] For what mattered was that the Abbé paid minute attention to his pupils, acquired their language (which had scarcely ever been done by the hearing before). And then, by associating signs with pictures and written words, he taught them to read; and with this, in one swoop, he opened to them the world's learning and culture. De l'Epée's system of "methodical" signs—a combination of their own Sign with signed French grammar—enabled deaf students to write down what was said to them through a signing interpreter, a method so successful that, for the first time, it enabled ordinary deaf pupils to read and write French, and thus acquire an education. His school, founded in 1755, was the first to achieve public support. He trained a multitude of teachers for the deaf, who, by the time of his death in 1789, had established twenty-one schools for the deaf in France and Europe. The future of de l'Epée's own school seemed uncertain during the turmoil of revolution, but by 1791 it had become the National Institution for Deaf-Mutes in Paris, headed by the brilliant grammarian Sicard. De l'Epée's own book, as revolutionary as Copernicus' in its own way, was first published in 1776.

De l'Epée's book, a classic, is available in many languages. But what have not been available, have been virtually unknown, are the equally important (and, in some ways, even more fascinating) original writings of the deaf—the first deaf-mutes ever able to write. Harlan Lane and Franklin Philip have done a great service in making these so readily available to us in *The Deaf Experience.* Especially moving and important are the 1779 "Observations" of Pierre Desloges—the first book to be published by a deaf person—now available in English for the first time. Desloges himself, deafened at an early age, and virtually without speech, provides us first with a frightening description of the world, or unworld, of the languageless.

At the beginning of my infirmity, and for as long as I was living apart from other deaf people . . . I was unaware of sign language. I used only scattered, isolated, and unconnected signs. I did not know the art of combining them to form distinct pictures with which one can represent various ideas, transmit them to one's peers, and converse in logical discourse.

Thus Desloges, though obviously a highly gifted man, could scarcely entertain "ideas," or engage in "logical discourse," *until* he had acquired sign language (which, as is usual with the deaf, he learned from someone deaf, in his case from an illiterate deaf-mute). Desloges, though highly intelligent, was intellectually disabled until he learned Sign—and, specifically, to use the word that the British neurologist Hughlings-Jackson was to use a century later in regard to the disabilities attendant on aphasia, he was unable to "propositionize." It is worth clarifying this by quoting Hughlings-Jackson's own words:[16]

> We do not either speak or think in words or signs only, but in words or signs referring to one another in a particular manner. . . . Without a proper interrelation of its parts, a verbal utterance would be a mere succession of names, a word-heap, embodying no proposition. . . . The unit of speech is a proposition. Loss of speech (aphasia) is, therefore, the loss of power to propositionize . . . not only loss of power to propositionize aloud (to talk), but to propositionize either internally or externally. . . . The speechless patient has lost speech, not only in the popular sense that he cannot speak aloud, but in the fullest sense. We speak not only to tell other people what we think, but to tell ourselves what we think. Speech is a part of thought.

This is why, earlier, I spoke of prelingual deafness as being potentially far more devastating than blindness. For it may dispose, unless this is averted, to a condition of being virtually without language—and of being unable to "propositionize"—which must be compared to aphasia, a condition in which thinking itself can become incoherent and stunted. The languageless deaf may indeed be *as if* imbecilic—and in a particularly cruel way, in that intelligence, though present and perhaps abundant, is locked up so long as the lack of language lasts. Thus the Abbé

Sicard is right, as well as poetic, when he writes of the introduction of Sign as "opening up the doors of . . . intelligence for the first time."

Nothing is more wonderful, or more to be celebrated, than something that will unlock a person's capacities and allow him to grow and think, and no one praises or portrays this with such fervor or eloquence as these suddenly liberated mutes, such as Pierre Desloges:

> The [sign] language we use among ourselves, being a faithful image of the object expressed, is singularly appropriate for making our ideas accurate and for extending our comprehension by getting us to form the habit of constant observation and analysis. This language is lively; it portrays sentiment, and develops the imagination. No other language is more appropriate for conveying strong and great emotions.

But even de l'Epée was unaware, or could not believe, that sign language was a complete language, capable of expressing not only every emotion but every proposition and enabling its users to discuss any topic, concrete or abstract, as economically and effectively and grammatically as speech.[17]

This indeed has always been evident, if only implicitly, to all native signers, but has always been denied by the hearing and speaking, who, however well intentioned, regard signing as something rudimentary, primitive, pantomimic, a poor thing. De l'Epée had this delusion—and it remains an almost universal delusion of the hearing now. On the contrary, it must be understood that Sign is the equal of speech, lending itself equally to the rigorous and the poetic—to philosophical analysis or to making love—indeed, with an ease that is sometimes greater than that of speech. (Indeed, if learned as a primary language, Sign may be used and maintained by the hearing as a continuing and at times preferred alternative to speech.)

The philosopher Condillac, who at first had seen deaf people as "sentient statues" or "ambulatory machines" incapable of thought or any connected mental activity, coming incognito to de l'Epée's classes, became a convert, and provided the first philosophic endorsement of his method and of sign language:

> From the language of action de l'Epée has created a methodical, simple, and easy art with which he gives his pupils ideas of every kind, and, I daresay, ideas more precise than the ones usually acquired with the help of hearing. When as children we are reduced to judging the meaning of words from the circumstances in which we hear them, it often happens that we grasp the meaning only approximately, and we are satisfied with this approximation all our lives. It is different with the deaf taught by de l'Epée. He has only one means for giving them sensory ideas; it is to analyze and to get the pupil to analyze with him. So he leads them from sensory to abstract ideas; we can judge how advantageous de l'Epée's action language is over the speech sounds of our governesses and tutors.

From Condillac to the public at large, who also flocked to de l'Epée's and Sicard's demonstrations, there came an enormous and generous change of heart, a welcoming of the previously outcast into human society. This period—which now seems a sort of golden period in deaf history—saw the rapid establishment of deaf schools, usually manned by deaf teachers, throughout the civilized world, the emergence of the deaf from neglect and obscurity, their emancipation and enfranchisement, and their rapid appearance in positions of eminence and responsibility—deaf writers, deaf engineers, deaf philosophers, deaf intellectuals, previously inconceivable, were suddenly possible.

When Laurent Clerc (a pupil of Massieu, himself a pupil of Sicard) came to the United States in 1816, he had an immediate and extraordinary impact, for American teachers up to this point had never been exposed to, never even imagined, a deaf-mute of impressive intelligence and education, had never imagined the possibilities dormant in the deaf. With Thomas Gallaudet, Clerc set up the American Asylum for the Deaf, in Hartford, in 1817.[18] As Paris—teachers, *philosophes*, and public-at-large—was moved, amazed, "converted" by de l'Epée in the 1770s, so America was to be converted fifty years later.

The atmosphere at the Hartford Asylum, and at other schools soon to be set up, was marked by the sort of enthusiasm and excitement only seen at the start of grand intellectual and humanitarian adventures.[19] The prompt and spectacular success of the Hartford Asylum soon led to the opening of other schools wherever there was sufficient density of population, and thus of deaf students. Virtually all the teachers of the deaf (nearly all of whom were fluent signers and many of whom were deaf) went to Hartford. The French sign system imported by Clerc rapidly amalgamated with the indigenous sign languages here—the deaf generate sign language wherever there are communities of deaf people; it is for them the easiest and most natural mode of communication—to form a uniquely expressive and powerful hybrid, American Sign Language (ASL).[20] A special indigenous strength—presented convincingly by Nora Ellen Groce in her book, *Everyone Here Spoke Sign Language*—was the contribution of the Martha's Vineyard deaf to the development of ASL. A substantial minority of the population there suffered from a hereditary deafness, and most of the island had adopted an easy and powerful sign language. Virtually all the deaf of the Vineyard were sent to the Hartford Asylum in its formative years, where they contributed to the developing national language the unique strength of their own.

One has, indeed, a strong sense of pollination, of people coming to and fro, bringing regional languages, with all their idiosyncrasies and strengths, to Hartford, and taking back an increasingly polished and generalized language.[21] The rise of deaf literacy and deaf education was as spectacular in the United States as it had been in France, and it soon spread to other parts of the world.

Lane estimates that by 1869 there were 550 teachers of the deaf worldwide and that 41 percent of the teachers of the deaf in the United States were themselves deaf. In 1864 Congress passed a law authorizing the Columbia Institution for the Deaf and the Blind in Washington to become a national deaf-mute college, the first institution of higher learning specifically for the deaf. Its first principal was Edward Gallaudet—the son of Thomas Gallaudet, who had brought Clerc to the United States in 1816. Gallaudet College, as it was later rechristened (it is now Gallaudet University), is still the only liberal arts college for deaf students in the world—though there are now several programs and institutes for the deaf associated with technical colleges. (The most famous of these is at the Rochester Institute of Technology, where there are more than 1,500 deaf students forming the National Technical Institute for the Deaf.)

The great impetus of deaf education and liberation, which

had swept France between 1770 and 1820, thus continued its triumphant course in the United States until 1870 (Clerc, immensely active to the end and personally charismatic, died in 1869). And then—and this is the turning point in the entire story—the tide turned, turned against the use of Sign by and for the deaf, so that within twenty years the work of a century was undone.

Indeed, what was happening with the deaf and Sign was part of a general (and if one wishes, "political") movement of the time: a trend to Victorian oppressiveness, and conformism, intolerance of minorities, and minority usages, of every kind—religious, linguistic, ethnic. Thus it was at this time that the "little nations" and "little languages" of the world (for example, Wales and Welsh) found themselves under pressure to assimilate or conform.

Specifically, there had been for two centuries a countercurrent of feeling, from teachers and parents of deaf children, that the goal of deaf education should be teaching the deaf how to speak. Already, a century earlier, de l'Epée had found himself in implicit if not explicit opposition to Pereire, the greatest "oralist" or "demutizer" of his time, who dedicated his life to teaching deaf people how to speak; this was a task, indeed, for which dedication was needed, for it required years of the most intensive and arduous training, with one teacher working with one pupil, to have any hope of success, whereas de l'Epée could educate pupils by the hundred. Now, in the 1870s, a current that had been growing for decades, fed, paradoxically, by the immense success of the deaf-mute asylums and their spectacular demonstrations of the educability of the deaf, erupted and attempted to eliminate the very instrument of success.

There were, indeed, real dilemmas, as there had always been, and they exist to this day. What good, it was asked, was the use of signs without speech? Would this not restrict deaf people, in daily life, to intercourse with other deaf people? Should not speech (and lipreading) be taught instead, allowing a full integration of the deaf into the general population? Should not signing be proscribed, lest it interfere with speech?[22]

But there is the other side of the argument. If the teaching of speech is arduous and occupies dozens of hours a week, might not its advantages be offset by these thousands of hours taken away from general education? Might one not end up with a functional illiterate who has, at best, a poor imitation of speech? What is "better," integration or education? Might one have both, by combining both speech and Sign? Or will any such attempted combination bring about, not the best, but the worst, of both worlds?

These dilemmas, these debates, of the 1870s seem to have been gathering force beneath the surface throughout a century of achievement—an achievement that could be seen, and was seen, by many, as perverse, as conducive to isolation and a set-apart people.

Edward Gallaudet himself was an open-minded man who traveled extensively in Europe in the late 1860s, touring deaf schools in fourteen countries. He found that the majority used both sign language and speech, that the sign language schools did as well as the oral schools as far as articulating speech was concerned, but obtained superior results in general education. He felt that articulation skills, though highly desirable, could not be the basis of primary instruction—that this had to be achieved, and achieved early, by Sign.

Gallaudet was balanced, but others were not. There had been a rash of "reformers"—Samuel Gridley Howe and Horace Mann were egregious examples—who clamored for an overthrow of the "old-fashioned" sign language asylums and for the introduction of "progressive" oralist schools. The Clarke School for the Deaf in Northampton, Massachusetts, was the first of these, opened in 1867. (It was the model and inspiration of the Northampton School in England, founded by the Reverend Thomas Arnold the following year.) But the most important and powerful of these "oralist" figures was Alexander Graham Bell, who was at once heir to a family tradition of teaching elocution and correcting speech impediments (his father and grandfather were both eminent in this), tied into a strange family mix of deafness denied (both his mother and his wife were deaf, but never acknowledged this) and, of course, a technological genius in his own right. When Bell threw all the weight of his immense authority and prestige into the advocacy of oralism, the scales were, finally, overbalanced and tipped, and at the notorious International Congress of Educators of the Deaf held at Milan in 1880, where deaf teachers were themselves excluded from the vote, oralism won the day and the use of Sign in schools was "officially" proscribed.[23] Deaf pupils were prohibited from using their own "natural" language, and thenceforth forced to learn, as best they might, the (for them) "unnatural" language of speech. And perhaps this was in keeping with the spirit of the age, its overweening sense of science as power, of commanding nature and never deferring to it.

One of the consequences of this was that hearing teachers, not deaf teachers, now had to teach deaf students. The proportion of deaf teachers for the deaf, which was close to 50 percent in 1850, fell to 25 percent by the turn of the century, and to 12 percent by 1960. More and more, English became the language of instruction for deaf students, taught by hearing teachers, fewer and fewer of whom knew any sign language at all—the situation depicted by David Wright, at his school in the 1920s.

None of this would have mattered had oralism worked. But the effect, unhappily, was the reverse of what was desired—an intolerable price was exacted for the acquisition of speech. Deaf students of the 1850s who had been to the Hartford Asylum, or other such schools, were highly literate and educated—fully the equal of their hearing counterparts. Today the reverse is true. Oralism and the suppression of Sign have resulted in a dramatic deterioration in the educational achievement of deaf children and in the literacy of the deaf generally.[24]

These dismal facts are known to all teachers of the deaf, however they are to be interpreted. Hans Furth, a psychologist whose work is concerned with cognition of the deaf, states that the deaf do as well as the hearing on tasks that measure intelligence without the need for acquired information. He argues that the congenitally deaf suffer from "information deprivation." There are a number of reasons for this. First, they are less exposed to the "incidental" learning that takes place out of school—for example, to that buzz of conversation that is the background of ordinary life; to television, unless it is captioned, etc. Second, the content of deaf education is meager compared to that of hearing children: so much time is spent teaching deaf children speech—one must envisage between five and eight years of intensive tutoring—that there is little time for transmitting information, culture, complex skills, or anything else.

Yet the desire to have the deaf speak, the insistence that they speak—and from the first, the odd superstitions that have always clustered around the use of sign language, to say nothing of the enormous investment in oral schools, allowed this deplorable situation to develop, practically unnoticed except by deaf people, who themselves being unnoticed had little to say in the matter. And it was only during the 1960s that historians and psychologists, as well as parents and teachers of deaf children, started asking, "What has happened? What *is* happening?" It was only in the 1960s and early 1970s that this situation reached the public, in the form of novels such as Joanne Greenberg's *In This Sign* and more recently the powerful play (and movie) *Children of a Lesser God* by Mark Medoff.[25]

There is the perception that something must be done. But what? Typically, there is the seduction of compromise—that a "combined" system, combining sign and speech, will allow the deaf to become adept at both. A further compromise, containing a deep confusion, is suggested: having a language intermediate between English and Sign (i.e., a signed English). This category of confusion goes back a long way—back to de l'Epée's "Methodical Signs," which were an attempt to intermediate between French and Sign. But true sign languages are in fact complete in themselves: their syntax, grammar, and semantics are complete, but they have a different character from that of any spoken or written language. Thus it is not possible to transliterate a spoken tongue into Sign word by word or phrase by phrase—their structures are essentially different. It is often imagined, vaguely, that sign language *is* English or French. It is nothing of the sort; it is itself, Sign. Thus, the "Signed English" now favored as a compromise is unnecessary, for no intermediary pseudo-language is needed. And yet, deaf people are forced to learn the signs not for the ideas and actions they want to express, but for phonetic English sounds they cannot hear.

Even now the use of signed English, in one form or another, is still favored against the use of ASL. Most teaching of the deaf, if done by signs, is done by signed English; most teachers of the deaf, if they know any sign, know this and not ASL; and the little cameos that appear on television screens all use signed English, not ASL. Thus, a century after the Milan conference, deaf people are still largely deprived of their own, indigenous language.

But what, more importantly, of the combined system by which students not only learn sign language but learn to lip-read and speak as well? Perhaps this is workable, if education takes account of which capacities are best developed at different phases of growth. The essential point is this: that profoundly deaf people show no native disposition whatever to speak. Speaking is an ability that must be taught them and is a labor of years. On the other hand, they show an immediate and powerful disposition to Sign, which as a visual language, is completely accessible to them. This is more apparent in the deaf children of deaf parents using Sign, who make their first signs when they are about six months old and have considerable sign fluency by the age of fifteen months.[26]

Language must be introduced and acquired as early as possible or its development may be permanently retarded and impaired, with all the problems in "propositionizing" which Hughlings-Jackson discussed. This can be done, with the profoundly deaf, only by Sign. Therefore deafness must be diagnosed as early as possible.[27] Deaf children must first be exposed to fluent signers, whether these be their parents, or teachers, or whoever. Once signing is learned—and it may be fluent by three years of age—

then all else may follow: a free intercourse of minds, a free flow
of information, the acquisition of reading and writing, and perhaps that of speech. There is no evidence that signing inhibits
the acquisition of speech. Indeed the reverse is probably so.

Have the deaf always and everywhere been seen as "handicapped" or "inferior"? Have they always suffered, must they
always suffer, segregation and isolation? Can one imagine their
situation otherwise? If only there were a world where being
deaf did not matter, and in which all deaf people could enjoy
complete fulfillment and integration! A world in which they
would not even be perceived as "handicapped" or "deaf."[28]

Such worlds do exist, and have existed in the past, and such a
world is portrayed in Nora Ellen Groce's beautiful and fascinating *Everyone Here Spoke Sign Language: Hereditary Deafness on
Martha's Vineyard.* Through a mutation, a recessive gene brought
out by inbreeding, a form of hereditary deafness existed for
250 years on Martha's Vineyard, Massachusetts, following
the arrival of the first deaf settlers in the 1690s. By the mid–
nineteenth century, scarcely an up-Island family was unaffected,
and in some villages (Chilmark, West Tisbury) the incidence of
deafness had risen to one in four. In response to this, the entire
community learned Sign, and there was free and complete
intercourse between the hearing and the deaf. Indeed the deaf
were scarcely seen as "deaf," and certainly not seen as being at
all "handicapped."[29]

In the astonishing interviews recorded by Groce, the island's
older residents would talk at length, vividly and affectionately,
about their former relatives, neighbors, and friends, usually
without even mentioning that they were deaf. And it would only
be if this question was specifically asked that there would be a

pause and then, "Now you come to mention it, yes, Ebenezer *was* deaf and dumb." But Ebenezer's deaf-and-dumbness had never set him apart, had scarcely even been noticed as such: he had been seen, he was remembered, simply as "Ebenezer"— friend, neighbor, dory fisherman—not as some special, handicapped, set-apart deaf-mute. The deaf on Martha's Vineyard loved, married, earned their livings, worked, thought, wrote, as everyone else did—they were not set apart in any way, unless it was that they were, on the whole, better educated than their neighbors, for virtually all of the deaf on Martha's Vineyard were sent to be educated at the Hartford Asylum—and were often looked at as the most sagacious in the community.[30]

Intriguingly, even after the last deaf Islander had died in 1952, the hearing tended to preserve Sign among themselves, not merely for special occasions (telling dirty jokes, talking in church, communicating between boats, etc.) but generally. They would slip into it, involuntarily, sometimes in the middle of a sentence, because Sign is "natural" to all who learn it (as a primary language), and has an intrinsic beauty and excellence sometimes superior to speech.[31]

I was so moved by Groce's book that the moment I finished it I jumped in the car, with only a toothbrush, a tape recorder, and a camera—I had to see this enchanted island for myself. I saw how some of the oldest inhabitants still preserved Sign, delighted in it, among themselves. My first sight of this, indeed, was quite unforgettable. I drove up to the old general store in West Tisbury on a Sunday morning and saw half a dozen old people gossiping together on the porch. They could have been any old folks, old neighbors, talking together—until suddenly, very startlingly, they all dropped into Sign. They signed for a minute, laughed, then dropped back into speech. At this moment I knew I had come to the right place. And, speaking to one of the very oldest there, I found one other thing, of very great interest. This old lady, in her nineties, but sharp as a pin, would sometimes fall into a peaceful reverie. As she did so, she might have seemed to be knitting, her hands in constant complex motion. But her daughter, also a signer, told me she was not knitting but thinking to herself, thinking in Sign. And even in sleep, I was further informed, the old lady might sketch fragmentary signs on the counterpane—she was dreaming in Sign. Such phenomena cannot be accounted as merely social. It is evident that if a person has learned Sign as a primary language, his brain/mind will retain this, and use it, for the rest of that person's life, even though hearing and speech be freely available and unimpaired. Sign, I was now convinced, was a fundamental language of the brain.

Thinking in Sign

I FIRST became interested in the deaf—their history, their predicament, their language, their culture—when I was sent Harlan Lane's books to review. In particular, I was haunted by descriptions of isolated deaf people who had failed to acquire any language whatever: their evident intellectual disabilities and, equally seriously, the mishaps in emotional and social development to which they might fall prey in the absence of any authentic language or communication. What is necessary, I wondered, for us to become complete human beings? Is our humanity, so-called, partly dependent on language? What happens to us if we fail to acquire any language? Does language develop spontaneously and naturally, or does it require contact with other human beings?

One way—a dramatic way—of exploring these topics is to look at human beings deprived of language; and deprivation of language, in the form of aphasia, has been a central preoccupation of neurologists since the 1860s: Hughlings-Jackson, Head, Goldstein, Luria all wrote extensively on it—and Freud too wrote a monograph in the 1890s. But aphasia is the deprivation of language (through a stroke or other cerebral accident) in an already formed mind, a completed individual. One might say that language has already done its work here (if it has work to do) in the formation of mind and character. If one is to explore the fundamental role of language, one needs to study not its loss after being developed, but its failure to develop.

And yet I found it difficult to imagine such things: I had patients who had lost language, patients with aphasia, but could not imagine what it might be like not to have acquired language to begin with.

Two years ago, at the Braefield School for the Deaf, I met Joseph, a boy of eleven who had just entered school for the first time—an eleven-year-old with no language whatever. He had been born deaf, but this had not been realized until he was in his fourth year.[1] His failure to talk, or understand speech, at the normal age was put down to "retardation," then to "autism," and these diagnoses had clung to him. When his deafness finally became apparent he was seen as "deaf and dumb," dumb not only literally, but metaphorically, and there was never any real attempt to teach him language.

Joseph longed to communicate, but could not. Neither speaking nor writing nor signing was available to him, only gesture and pantomime, and a marked ability to draw. What has happened to him? I kept asking myself. What is going on inside, how has he come to such a pass? He looked alive and animated, but profoundly baffled: his eyes were attracted to speaking mouths and signing hands—they darted to our mouths and hands, inquisitively, uncomprehendingly, and, it seemed to me, yearningly. He perceived that something was "going on" between us, but he could not comprehend what it was—he had, as yet, almost no idea of symbolic communication, of what it was to have a symbolic currency, to exchange meaning.

Previously deprived of opportunity—for he had never been exposed to Sign—and undermined in motive and affect (above all, the joy that play and language should give), Joseph was now just beginning to pick up a little Sign, beginning to have some communication with others. This, manifestly, gave him great joy; he wanted to stay at school all day, all night, all weekend, all the time. His distress at leaving school was painful to see, for going home meant, for him, return to the silence, return to a hopeless communicational vacuum, where he could have no converse, no commerce, with his parents, neighbors, friends; it meant being overlooked, becoming a nonperson, again.

This was very poignant, extraordinary—without any exact parallel in my experience. I was partly reminded of a two-year-old infant trembling on the verge of language—but Joseph was eleven, was like an eleven-year-old in most other ways. I was partly reminded in a way of a nonverbal animal, but no animal ever gave the feeling of yearning for language as Joseph did. Hughlings-Jackson, it came to me, once compared aphasics to dogs—but dogs seem complete and contented in their languagelessness, whereas the aphasic has a tormenting sense of loss. And Joseph, too: he clearly had an anguished sense of something missing, a sense of his own crippledness and deficit. He made me think of wild children, feral children, though clearly he was not "wild" but a creature of our civilization and habits—but one who was nonetheless radically cut off.

Joseph was unable, for example, to communicate how he had spent the weekend—one could not really ask him, even in Sign: he could not even grasp the *idea* of a question, much less formulate an answer. It was not only language that was missing: there was not, it was evident, a clear sense of the past, of "a day ago" as distinct from "a year ago." There was a strange lack of historical sense, the feeling of a life that lacked autobiographical and historical dimension, the feeling of a life that only existed in the moment, in the present.

His visual intelligence—his ability to solve visual puzzles and problems—was good, in radical contrast to his profound difficulties with verbally based problems. He could draw and liked drawing: he did good diagrams of the room, he enjoyed drawing people; he "got" cartoons, he "got" visual concepts. It was this that above all gave me the feeling of intelligence, but an intelligence largely confined to the visual. He "picked up" tic-tac-toe and was soon very good at it; I had the sense that he might readily learn checkers or chess.

Joseph saw, distinguished, categorized, used; he had no problems with *perceptual* categorization or generalization, but he could not, it seemed, go much beyond this, hold abstract ideas in mind, reflect, play, plan. He seemed completely literal—unable to judge images or hypotheses or possibilities, unable to enter an imaginative or figurative realm. And yet, one still felt, he was of normal intelligence, despite these manifest limitations of intellectual functioning. It was not that he lacked a mind, but that he was not *using his mind fully*.

It is clear that thought and language have quite separate (biological) origins, that the world is examined and mapped and responded to long before the advent of language, that there is a huge range of thinking—in animals, or infants—long before the emergence of language. (No one has examined this more beautifully than Piaget, but it is obvious to every parent—or pet lover.) A human being is not mindless or mentally deficient without language, but he is severely restricted in the range of his thoughts, confined, in effect, to an immediate, small world.[2]

For Joseph, the beginnings of a communication, a language, had now started, and he was tremendously excited at this. The school had found that it was not just formal instruction that he needed, but playing with language, language games, as with a toddler learning language for the first time. In this, it was hoped, he might begin to acquire language and conceptual thinking, to acquire it in the *act* of intellectual play. I found myself thinking of the twins Luria described, who had been in a sense so "retarded" because their language was so bad, and how they improved, immeasurably, when they acquired it.[3] Would this too be possible for Joseph?

The very word "infant" means nonspeaking, and there is much to suggest that the acquisition of language marks an absolute and qualitative development in human nature. Though a well-developed, active, bright eleven-year-old, Joseph was in this sense still an infant—denied the power, the world, that language opens up. In Joseph Church's words:

> Language opens up new orientations and new possibilities for learning and for action, dominating and transforming pre-verbal experiences. . . . Language is not just one function among many . . . but an all-pervasive characteristic of the individual such that he becomes a *verbal organism* (all of whose experiences and actions and conceptions are now altered in accordance with a verbalized or symbolic experience).
>
> Language transforms experience. . . . Through language . . . one can induct the child into a purely symbolic realm of past and future, of remote places, of ideal relationships, of hypothetical events, of imaginative literature, of imaginary entities ranging from werewolves to pi-mesons. . . .

At the same time the learning of language transforms the individual in such a way that he is enabled to do new things for himself, or to do old things in new ways. Language permits us to deal with things at a distance, to act on them without physically handling them. First, we can act on other people, or on objects through people. . . . Second, we can manipulate symbols in ways impossible with the things they stand for, and so arrive at novel and even creative versions of reality. . . . We can verbally rearrange situations which in themselves would resist rearrangement . . . we can isolate features which in fact cannot be isolated . . . we can juxtapose objects and events far separated in time and space . . . we can, if we will, turn the universe symbolically inside out.

We can do this, but Joseph could not. Joseph could not reach that symbolic plane which is the normal human birthright from earliest childhood on. He seemed, like an animal, or an infant, to be stuck in the present, to be confined to literal and immediate perception, though made aware of this by a consciousness that no infant could have.[4]

I began to wonder about other deaf people who had reached adolescence, adulthood perhaps, without language of any kind. They had existed, in considerable numbers, in the eighteenth century: Jean Massieu was one of the most famous of these. Languageless until the age of almost fourteen, Massieu then became a pupil of the Abbé Sicard and achieved a spectacular success, becoming eloquent both in Sign and written French. Massieu himself wrote a short autobiography, while Sicard wrote an entire book about him, of how it was possible to "liberate" the languageless into a new form of being.[5] Massieu described his growing up on a farm with eight brothers and sisters, five of whom were, like himself, born deaf:

> Until the age of thirteen and nine months I remained at home without ever receiving any education. I was totally unlettered. I expressed my ideas by manual signs and gestures . . . the signs I used to express my ideas to my family were quite different from the signs of educated deaf-mutes. Strangers did not understand us when we expressed our ideas with signs, but the neighbors did. . . . Children my own age would not play with me, they looked down on me, I was like a dog. I passed the time alone playing with a top or a mallet and ball, or walking on stilts.

It is not entirely clear what Massieu's mind was like, given the absence of a genuine language (though it is clear that he had plenty of communication of a primitive sort, using the "home signs" that he and his deaf siblings had devised, which constituted a complex, but almost grammarless, gestural system).[6] He tells us:

> I saw cattle, horses, donkeys, pigs, dogs, cats, vegetables, houses, fields, grapevines, and after seeing all these things remembered them well.

He also had a sense of numbers, even though he lacked names for these:

> Before my education I did not know how to count; my fingers had taught me. I did not know numbers; I counted on my fingers, and when the count went beyond ten I made notches on a stick.

And he tells us, very poignantly, how he envied other children going to school; how he took up books, but could make nothing of them; and how he tried to copy the letters of the alphabet with a quill, knowing that they must have some strange power, but unable to give any meaning to them.

Sicard's description of Massieu's education is fascinating. He found (as I had observed with Joseph) that the boy had a good eye; and he started by drawing pictures of objects and asking Massieu to do the same. Then, to introduce Massieu to language, Sicard wrote the names of the objects on their pictures. At first, his pupil "was utterly mystified. He had no idea how lines that did not appear to picture anything could function as an image for objects and represent them with such accuracy and speed." Then, very suddenly, Massieu *got* it, got the idea of an abstract and symbolic representation: "at that moment [he] learned the whole advantage and difficulty of writing . . . [and] from that moment on, the drawing was banished, we replaced it with writing."

Now Massieu perceived that an object, or an image, might be represented by a *name*, he developed a tremendous, violent hunger for names. Sicard gives marvelous descriptions of how the two of them took walks together, with Massieu demanding and noting the names for everything:

We visited an orchard to name all the fruits. We went into a woods to distinguish the oak from the elm . . . the willow from the poplar, eventually all the other inhabitants. . . . He didn't have enough tablets and pencils for all the names with which I filled his dictionary, and his soul seemed to expand and grow with these innumerable denominations. . . . Massieu's visits were those of a landowner seeing his rich domain for the first time.

With the acquisition of names, of words for everything, Sicard felt, there was a radical change in Massieu's relation to the world—he became like Adam: "This newcomer to earth was a stranger on his own estates, which were being restored to him as he learned their names."

If we ask: Why did Massieu demand all these names? Or why did Adam, even though he was alone at the time? Why did naming give Massieu such joy, and cause his soul to expand and grow? How did they alter his relation to the things previously nameless, so that now he felt that he owned them, that they had become his "domain"? What is naming *for?* It has to do, surely, with the primal power of words, to define, to enumerate, to allow mastery and manipulation; to move from the realm of objects and images to the world of concepts and names. A drawing of an oak tree depicts a particular tree, but the name "oak" denotes the entire class of oak trees, a general identity— "oakhood"—that applies to all oaks. Giving names, then, for Massieu, as he walked the woods, was his first grasp of a generalizing power that could transform the entire world; in this way, at the age of fourteen, he entered into the human estate, could know the world as home, the world as his "domain" in a way he had never known before.[7]

L. S. Vygotsky writes in *Thought and Language:*

A word does not refer to a single object but to a group or class of objects. Each word is therefore already a generalization. Generalization is a verbal act of thought and reflects reality in quite another way than sensation and perception reflect it.

He goes on to speak of the "dialectic leap" between sensation and thought, a leap that requires the achievement of "a *generalized* reflection of reality, which is also the essence of word meaning."[8]

Thus, for Massieu, nouns, names, nominals came first. Qualifying adjectives were needed, but these presented problems.

> Massieu did not wait for the adjectives, but made use of names of objects in which he found the salient quality he wanted to affirm of another object. . . . To express the swiftness of one of his comrades in a race, he said, "Albert is *bird*"; to express strength, he said, "Paul is *lion*"; for gentleness, he said, "Deslyons is *lamb*."

Sicard at first allowed and encouraged this, and then, "reluctantly," started to substitute adjectives ("gentle" for "lamb," "sweet" for "turtledove"), adding, "I consoled him for the goods that I had stolen from him . . . [explaining] that the additional words I was giving him were [equivalent] to those I was demanding that he abandon."[9]

Pronouns also gave particular problems. "He" was at first mistaken for a proper name; "I" and "you" were confused (as often happens with toddlers); but finally they were understood. Propositions aroused especial difficulties, but once grasped were seized with explosive force, so that suddenly Massieu found himself able (in Hughlings-Jackson's term) to "propositionize." Geometrical abstractions—invisible constructs—were the hardest of all. It was easy for Massieu to put square objects together, but a different achievement entirely for him to grasp squareness as a geometrical construct, to grasp the *idea* of a square.[10] This, in particular, aroused Sicard's enthusiasm: "Abstraction has been achieved! Another step! Massieu understands abstractions!" exulted Sicard. "He is a human creature."

Several months after seeing Joseph, I happened to reread the story of *Kaspar Hauser*, subtitled "An account of an individual kept in a dungeon, separated from all communication with the world, from early childhood to about the age of seventeen."[11] Though Kaspar's situation was far more bizarre and extreme, he reminded me of Joseph in a way. Kaspar, a young boy of about sixteen, was discovered one day in 1828, stumbling down a street in Nuremberg. He had with him a letter telling something of his strange history: how he had been given away by his mother, when six months old—she was penniless and her husband was dead—to a day-laborer with ten children. For reasons that never became clear, this foster father confined Kaspar in a cellar—he was chained, seated, and could not stand—without any communication or human contact for more than a dozen years. When he needed to be toileted or changed, his father-jailer put opium in his food and did what was necessary while Kaspar was unconscious in drug-sleep.

When he "came into the world" (this expression was often used by Kaspar to "designate his first exposure in Nuremberg, and his first awakening to the consciousness of mental life"), he rapidly learned that "there existed men and other creatures," and fairly rapidly—it took several months—started to acquire language. This awakening to human contact, this awakening to the world of shared meanings, of language, led to a sudden and brilliant awakening of his whole mind and soul. There was a

tremendous expansion and flowering of mental powers—
everything excited his wonder and joy, there was a boundless
curiosity, an incandescent interest in everything, a "love-affair
with the world." (Such a rebirth, a psychological birth, as
Leonard Shengold points out, is no more than a special, exag-
gerated, almost explosive form of what normally occurs in the
third year of life, with the discovery and emergence of language.) Kaspar showed, at first, a prodigious power of perception and memory, but the perception and memory were all for
particulars—he seemed both brilliant and incapable of abstract
thought. But as he acquired language he acquired the ability to
generalize, and with this moved from a world of innumerable
unconnected particulars to a connected, intelligible, and intelligent world.

This sudden, exuberant explosion of language and intelligence is essentially similar to what happened with Massieu—it
is what happens with the mind and soul if they have been
imprisoned (without being completely destroyed) from early
life, and the doors of the prison are suddenly thrown open.[12]

Cases like Massieu's must have been far commoner in the eighteenth century, when there was no compulsory schooling, but
they still occur occasionally even now, especially, perhaps in isolated rural environments or if the child has been misdiagnosed
and institutionalized from an early age.[13]

Indeed, in November of 1987 I received an extraordinary letter, from Susan Schaller, a sign language interpreter and
scholar from San Francisco.

Currently [wrote Schaller] I am writing an account of a
twenty-seven-year-old, prelingual, deaf man's successful

acquisition of his first language. He was born deaf and had never been exposed to any language, including sign language. My student, who had never communicated with another human for twenty-seven years (except for concrete and functional expressions via mime), amazingly survived his life of "solitary confinement" without his personality disintegrating.

Ildefonso was born on a farm in southern Mexico; he and a congenitally deaf brother were the only deaf members of his family and community, and they never had any schooling or contact with Sign. He worked as a migrant farm laborer, crossing in and out of the United States with various relatives. Although good-natured, he was essentially isolated, since he could make virtually no communication (other than gestural) with another human being. When he was first seen by Schaller, he seemed alert and alive, but fearful and bewildered, and with a sort of yearning and searching—somewhat as I had seen Joseph. He was, like Joseph, very observant ("he watches everything and everyone")—but, so to speak, observing from the outside, enthralled by, but not privy to, the inner world of language. When Schaller signed "Your name?" he simply copied the sign; this was all he would do at first, without the least comprehension that it *was* a sign.

The repetition of movements and sounds, as Schaller tried to teach Sign to Ildefonso, continued without any sense that they had an "inside," had meaning—there seemed a possibility that he would never get past this "mimetic echolalia," never enter the world of thought or language. And then, quite suddenly and unexpectedly, one day he did. The first breakthrough for Ildefonso, fascinatingly, was with numbers. All at once, he grasped what they were, how to operate with them, their *sense;* and this caused a sort of intellectual explosion, a grasping within days of the cardinal principles of arithmetic. There was still no concept of language (arithmetical symbolism, perhaps, is not a language, is not denotative in the same sense as words). But the acquisition of numbers, the mental operations of arithmetic, set his mind going, created a region of order in the chaos, and turned him for the first time to a sort of understanding and hope.[14]

The real breakthrough occurred on the sixth day, after hundreds and thousands of repetitions of words, in particular of the sign for "cat." Suddenly it was not just a movement to be copied, but a sign pregnant with meaning that could be used to symbolize a concept. This moment of understanding was intensely exciting and led to another intellectual explosion, not of something purely abstract (like the principles of arithmetic) this time, but of the sense and meaning of the world:

> His face stretches and opens with excitement . . . slowly at first, then hungrily, he sucks in everything, as though he had never seen it before: the door, the bulletin board, chairs, tables, students, the clock, the green blackboard and me. . . . He has entered the universe of humanity, he has discovered the communion of minds. He now knows that he and a cat and the table have names.

Schaller compares Ildefonso's "cat" with Helen Keller's "water"—the first word, the first sign, that leads to all others, that opens the imprisoned mind and intelligence.

This moment and the succeeding weeks were for Ildefonso a time of turning to the world with an enthralled new attention, an awakening, a birth, to the world of thought and language, after the merely perceptual existence of decades. The first two months were above all—for him, as for Massieu—months of naming, of defining the world and relating himself to it in an entirely new way. But, as with Kaspar Hauser, striking problems remained: in particular, as Schaller notes, "time concepts seemed impossible for him to grasp, units of time, tenses, temporal relationships, and just the idea of measuring time as events—took months to teach," and these were only gradually resolved.

Now, several years later, Ildefonso has acquired reasonably competent Sign, has met other deaf signers, and has joined their linguistic community. With this he has acquired, as Sicard said of Massieu, "a new being."

Joseph and Ildefonso, in their languagelessness, are extreme (but illuminating) cases: virtually all prelingually deaf people acquire *some* language in childhood, although it is often acquired late and markedly defective. There is a huge range of linguistic competence in the deaf; Joseph and Ildefonso represent one end of this spectrum. I found it impossible to ask Joseph a question—and this sort of linguistic deficiency may be widespread among deaf children, even those with some competence in Sign. This is a central observation of Isabelle Rapin:[15]

Asking questions of [deaf] children about what they had just read made me aware that many have a remarkable linguistic deficiency. They do not possess the linguistic device provided by the question forms. It is not that they do not know the answer to the question, it is that they do not understand the question. . . . I once asked a boy, "Who lives in your house?" (The question was translated to the boy in sign language by his teacher.) The boy had a blank look on his face. I then noted the teacher turned the question around into a series of declarative sentences: "In your house you, mother . . ." A look of comprehension came onto his face and he drew me a picture of his house with all family members, including the dog. . . . I noted again and again that teachers tended to hesitate to put questions to their pupils, and often expressed queries as incomplete sentences in which the deaf children could fill in the blanks.

It is not just question forms that are so lacking in the deaf—though lack of question forms, as Rapin says, is particularly pernicious, as it leads to the lack of information—it is the lack of language skills, and indeed language competence, that is so remarkable in prelingually deaf schoolchildren, a lack both lexical and grammatical. I was struck by the small vocabulary of many of the children I saw in Joseph's school, their naïveté, their concreteness of thought, their difficulties in reading and writing, and their ignorance of the world, an ignorance unimaginable in a normally intelligent child with hearing. My first thought, indeed, was that they were *not* normally intelligent, but had some peculiar, associated mental deficiency. And yet, I was assured, and my own observations told me, that these were not mentally deficient children in the ordinary sense of the word; they had the same range of intelligence as normal, but their intelligence, or certain aspects of it, was being undermined in some way. And not only intelligence: many of the children were passive or shy, lacking spontaneity, confidence, social ease—they seemed less animated, less playful than they should be.

I was dismayed by my glimpse of Joseph's school, Braefield. Like Joseph, the school itself is in some ways an extreme example (though in others it is distressingly close to the average). Most of the children there come from disadvantaged homes where there is poverty and unemployment and uprootedness in addition to deafness. And, importantly, Braefield is no longer a residential school; its children must leave at the end of the day, to go back to homes where parents cannot communicate with them; where the TV, uncaptioned, is unintelligible; where they cannot pick up basic information about the world.

And, indeed, other schools have given me a quite different impression. Thus at the chiefly residential California School for the Deaf in Fremont, many of the students have reasonable reading and writing skills, almost comparable to hearing students, whereas students at Braefield, more typically, average only a fourth-grade reading level at graduation. Many of the children at Fremont have larger vocabularies, sign well, are full of curiosity and questions, speak (or, more often, sign) fully and freely, have a sense of self-confidence and power of a sort I scarcely saw in Braefield. I was not surprised to hear of how well they did academically (far better than the average, scholastically retarded deaf).

Many factors seem to be at work here. On the whole, the children at Fremont come from more secure homes and backgrounds. A relatively high percentage of the teachers themselves are deaf: Fremont is one of the few schools in the United States with a policy of employing deaf teachers—such teachers are not only native signers but can transmit deaf culture and a positive image of deafness to the children. There is—and it is this that is so dramatically different from what I saw at Braefield— over and above the formal schooling, a community of children living together, signing together, playing together, sharing lives and meanings. Finally, there is an unusually high proportion of children with deaf parents at Fremont—these generally constitute less than 10 percent of deaf children. Acquiring Sign as a native language from infancy, these children have never known the tragedy of noncommunication with their parents that is often the lot of the profoundly deaf. In a residential school, these natively signing children are the chief introducers of the deaf world and its language to the deaf children of hearing parents; thus, there is far less of the isolation I was so struck by at Braefield.

If some deaf children do so much better than others, despite the same profound deafness, then it cannot be deafness as such that is producing problems but rather some of the *consequences* of deafness—in particular, difficulties or distortions in communicative life from the start. It cannot be pretended that Fremont is average; Braefield, alas, gives a better picture of the average situation of deaf children. But Fremont does show what, in ideal circumstances, deaf children can achieve; and it shows that it is not their innate linguistic or intellectual powers that are at fault, but rather obstructions to the normal development of these.

A visit to the Lexington School for the Deaf in New York was different again. For the population here, while not as disadvantaged as that of Braefield, lacked the peculiar advantages of Fremont (viz., a high proportion of deaf parents and a large deaf community). Yet I saw many (prelingually) deaf adolescents who had been, according to their teachers, almost languageless, or linguistically incompetent, in childhood, who were now doing very well—doing physics or creative writing, for instance, quite as well as hearing students. These children had been disabled earlier, and at great risks of permanent linguistic and intellectual disability, but had gone on—with intensive education—to attain good language and good communication in spite of this.

What emerges from the stories of Joseph and Ildefonso and others like them is a sense of peril—the especial peril that threatens human development, both intellectual and emotional, if the healthy acquisition of language fails to occur. In an extreme case there may be a complete failure in the acquisition of language, complete incomprehension of the idea of language. And language, as Church reminds us, is not just another faculty or skill, it is what makes thought possible, what separates thought from nonthought, what separates the human from the nonhuman.

None of us can remember how we "acquired" language; St. Augustine's description is a beautiful myth.[16] Nor are we, as parents, called on to "teach" our children language; they acquire it, or seem to, in the most automatic way, through virtue of being children, our children, and the communicative exchanges between us.

It is customary to distinguish grammar, verbal meanings, and communicative intent—the syntax, the semantics, the pragmatics of language—but as Bruner and others remind us, these always go together in the learning and use of language; and therefore, it is not language but language *use* we must study. The *first* language use, the first communication, is usually between mother and child, and language is acquired, arises, *between* the two.

One is born with one's senses; these are "natural." One can develop motor skills, naturally, by oneself. But one cannot acquire language by oneself; *this* skill comes in a unique category. It is impossible to acquire language without some essential innate ability, but this ability is only activated by another person who already possesses linguistic power and competence. It is only through transaction (or, as Vygotsky would say, "negotiation") with another that the language is achieved. (Wittgenstein writes in general terms of the "language games" we must all learn to play, and Brown speaks of "the original word game" played by mother and child.)

The mother—or father, or teacher, or indeed anyone who talks with the child—leads the infant step by step to higher levels of language; she leads him into language, and into the world picture it embodies (*her* world-picture, because it is her language; and beyond this, the world-picture of the culture she belongs to). The mother must always be a step ahead, in what Vygotsky calls the "zone of proximal development"; the infant cannot move into, or conceive of, the next stage ahead except through its being occupied and communicated to him by his mother.

But the mother's words, and the world behind them, would have no sense for the infant unless they corresponded to something in his own experience. He has an independent experience of the world given to him by his senses, and it is this which forms a correlation or confirmation of the mother's language, and in turn, is given meaning by it. It is the mother's language, internalized by the child, that allows it to move from sensation into "sense," to ascend from a perceptual into a conceptual world.

Social and emotional intercourse, intellectual intercourse too, starts from the first day of life.[17] Vygotsky was greatly interested in these prelinguistic, preintellectual stages of life, but his especial interest was in language and thought and how they come together in the development of the child. Vygotsky never forgets that language is always, and at once, both social and intellectual in function, nor does he forget for a moment the relation of intellect and affect, of how all communication, all thought, is also emotional, reflecting "the personal needs and interests, the inclinations and impulses" of the individual.

The corollary to all this is that if communication goes awry, it will affect intellectual growth, social intercourse, language development, and emotional attitudes, all at once, simultaneously and inseparably. And this, of course, is what may happen, what does happen, all too frequently, when a child is born deaf. Thus Hilde Schlesinger and Kathryn Meadow say, as the first sentence of their book, *Sound and Sign:*[18]

Profound childhood deafness is more than a medical diagnosis; it is a cultural phenomenon in which social, emotional, linguistic, and intellectual patterns and problems are inextricably bound together.

It is to Schlesinger and her colleagues, over the last twenty years, that we owe the fullest and deepest observations on the problems that may beset the deaf from childhood to adult life, and how these are related to the earliest communications between mother and child (and later, between teacher and pupil)—communications all too often grossly defective or distorted. Schlesinger's central concern is with how children—and, in particular, deaf children—are "coaxed" from a perceptual to a conceptual world, how crucially dependent this is upon such a dialogue. She has shown how the "dialectic leap" that Vygotsky speaks of—the leap from sensation to thought—involves not just talking, but the right *sort* of talking, a dialogue rich in communicative intent, in mutuality, and in the right sort of questioning, if the child is to make this great leap successfully.

Recording the conversational transactions of mother and child from earliest life, she has shown how often, and with what dire effects, this may go wrong when the child is deaf. Children, healthy children, are endlessly curious: they are constantly seeking cause and meaning, constantly asking "Why?" "How?" "What if?" It was the absence of such questioning, and the very incomprehension of such question forms, that struck so ominous a note when I visited Braefield. Writing in more general terms about the all-too-common problems of the deaf, Schlesinger notes:[19]

> At eight years of age, many deaf youngsters show a delay in their understanding of questions, still continue to label, do not impose "central meanings" to their answers. They have a poor sense of causation, and rarely introduce ideas about the future.

Many, but not all. There tends, indeed, to be a rather sharp distinction between children who have these problems and those who do not, between those who are intellectually, linguistically, socially, and emotionally "normal" and those who are not. This distinction, so different from the normal bell-curve distribution of abilities, shows that the dichotomy occurs after birth, that there must be early life experiences with a decisive power to determine the entire future. The origin of questioning, of an active and questing disposition in the mind, is not something that arises spontaneously, *de novo*, or directly from the impact of experience; it stems, it is stimulated, by communicative

exchange—it requires *dialogue*, in particular the complex dialogue of mother and child.[20] It is here, Schlesinger finds, that
the dichotomies start:[21]

> Mothers talk with their children, do so very differently, and
> tend to be more often at one side or the other of a series of
> dichotomies. Some talk *with* their youngsters and participate
> primarily in dialogue; some primarily talk *at* their children.
> Some mainly support the actions of their offspring, and if not,
> provide reasons why not; others primarily control the actions
> of their children, and do not explain why. Some ask gen-
> uine questions ... others constraint questions. . . . Some are
> prompted by what the child says or does; others by their own
> inner needs and interests. . . . Some describe a large world in
> which events happened in the past and will happen in the
> future; others comment only about the here and now. . . .
> Some mothers mediate the environment by endowing stimuli
> with meaning [and others do not].

A terrible power, it would seem, lies with the mother to communicate with her child properly or not; to introduce probing
questions such as "How?" "Why?" and "What if?" or replace
them with a mindless monologue of "What's this?" "Do that"; to
communicate a sense of logic and causality, or to leave everything at the dumb level of unaccountability; to introduce a vivid
sense of place or time, or to refer only to the here and now; to
introduce a "generalized reflection of reality," a conceptual
world that will give coherence and meaning to life, and chal-
lenge the mind and emotions of the child, or to leave everything
at the level of the ungeneralized, the unquestioned, at something almost below the animal level of the perceptual.[22] Chil-

dren, it would seem, cannot choose the world they will live in—
the mental and emotional, any more than the physical world;
they are dependent, in the beginning, on what they are introduced to by their mothers.

It is not just language, but thought, that must be introduced.
Otherwise the child will remain helplessly trapped in a concrete
and perceptual world—the situation with Joseph, Kaspar, and
Ildefonso. This peril is much greater if the child is deaf—
because (hearing) parents may not know how to address their
child and, if they communicate at all, may use rudimentary
forms of dialogue and language that do not advance the child's
mind and that, indeed, prevent its advance.

Children seem to copy faithfully the cognitive world (and
"style") introduced to them by their mothers [Schlesinger
writes]. Some mothers introduce a world that is populated
by individual, static objects in the here-and-now labelled in
identical ways for their children from toddlerhood through
latency. . . . Such mothers avoid language at a distance from
the perceptual world . . . and in poignant attempts to share a
world with their offspring join, and remain in, the perceptual
world of their children. . . .

[Other mothers, in contrast], introduce a world wherein
things that are seen, touched and heard are enthusiastically
processed through language. The world they introduce is
wider, more complex, and more interesting to the toddlers.
They too label objects in the perceptual world of their children, but use correct labels for more sophisticated percepts,
and add attributes to them via adjectives. . . . They include
people, and label the actions and feelings of individuals in the
world, and characterize them via adverbs. They not only

describe the perceptual world but help their children *reorganize* it and to *reason* about its multiple possibilities.[23]

These mothers, then, encourage the formation of a conceptual world which, far from impoverishing, enhances the perceptual world, enriching it and elevating it continually to the level of symbol and meaning. Poor dialogue, communication defeat, so Schlesinger feels, leads not only to intellectual constriction but to timidity and passivity; creative dialogue, a rich communicative interchange in childhood, awakens the imagination and mind, leads to a self-sufficiency, a boldness, a playfulness, a humor, that will be with the person for the rest of his life.[24]

Charlotte, a little girl of six, is also, like Joseph, congenitally deaf. But Charlotte is tremendously animated, playful, full of curiosity, turned vividly to the world. She is almost indistinguishable from any other six-year-old—totally different from poor, cut-off Joseph. What made the difference? As soon as Charlotte's parents realized she was deaf—when she was a few months old—they decided to learn a signed language, knowing that she would not be able to pick up spoken language easily. They did this, as did several of their relatives and friends. As Charlotte's mother, Sarah Elizabeth, wrote when Charlotte was four:

Our daughter Charlotte was diagnosed profoundly deaf at ten months old. During these past three years we have experienced a range of emotions: disbelief, panic and anxiety, rage, depression and grief, and finally acceptance and appreciation. As our initial panic wore off it became clear that we needed to use sign language with our daughter while she was young.[25]

We started a sign language class at our home studying

Signed Exact English, SEE, an exact replication of spoken English in signs, which we felt would help us in passing on our English language, literature, and culture to our child. As hearing parents we were overwhelmed by the task of learning a new language ourselves and having to teach it to Charlotte simultaneously, so the familiarity of English syntax made sign language seem accessible to us. . . . We desperately wanted to believe Charlotte was similar to us.

After a year we decided to move away from the rigidity of SEE to pidgin Signed English, a mixture of American Sign Language vocabulary, which is more visually descriptive, and English syntax, which is familiar . . . [but] the elaborate linear structures of spoken English don't translate into interesting sign language, so we had to reorient the way we thought to produce visual sentences. We were introduced to the most lively and exciting aspects of signing: idioms, humor, mime, whole-concept signs, and facial expression. . . . Now we are moving to American Sign Language, studying it with a deaf woman, a native signer who can communicate in signs without hesitation and can codify the language for us hearing people. We are excited and stimulated by the process of learning an ingenious and sensible language which has such beauty and imagination. It is a delight to realize that Charlotte's signing reflects visual thought patterns. We are startled into thinking differently about physical objects, and their placement and motion, because of Charlotte's expressions.

I found this narrative powerful and fascinating, indicating how Charlotte's parents first wanted to believe their daughter essentially similar to themselves, despite the fact that she uses her eyes, not her ears; how they first used SEE, which has no real structure of its own, but is a mere transliteration of an auditory language, and how they only gradually came to appreciate the fundamental visuality of their child, her use of "visual thought patterns," and how this both needed and generated a visual language. Rather than imposing their auditory world on their child, as so many parents of the deaf do, they encouraged her to advance into her own (visual) world, which they were then able to share with her. By the age of four, indeed, Charlotte had advanced so far into visual thinking and language that she was able to provide new ways of thinking—revelations—to her parents.

Early in 1987, Charlotte and her family moved from California to Albany, New York, and her mother wrote again to me:

Charlotte is now a six-year-old first-grader. We, of course, feel she is a remarkable person because, although profoundly deaf, she is interested, thoughtful, competent within her (mainly) hearing world. She seems comfortable in both ASL and English, communicates enthusiastically with deaf adults and children and reads and writes at a third-grade level. Her hearing brother, Nathaniel, is fluent and easy in Sign; our family conducts many conversations and much business in sign language. . . . I feel our experience bears out the idea that early exposure to visually coherent language develops complex conceptual thought processes. Charlotte knows how to think and how to reason. She uses effectively the linguistic tools she has been given to build complicated ideas.

When I went to visit Charlotte and her family, the first thing that struck me was that they *were* a family—full of fun, full of liveliness, full of questions, all together. There was none of the isolation one so often sees with the deaf—and none of the "primitive" language ("What's this? What's that? Do this! Do that!"), the condescension, of which Schlesinger speaks. Charlotte herself was full of questions, full of curiosity, full of life—a delightful, imaginative, and playful child, vividly turned to the world and to others. She was disappointed that I did not sign, but instantly commandeered her parents as interpreters and questioned me closely about the wonders of New York.

About thirty miles from Albany is a forest and river, and here I later drove with Charlotte, her parents, and her brother. Charlotte loves the natural world as much as the human world, but loves it in an intelligent way. She had an eye for different habitats, for the way things live together; she perceived cooperation and competition, the dynamics of existence. She was fascinated by the ferns that grew by the river, saw that they were very different from the flowers, understood the distinction between spores and seeds. She would exclaim excitedly in Sign over all the shapes and colors, but then attend and pause to ask, "How?" and "Why?" and "What if?" Clearly, it was not isolated facts that she wanted, but connections, understanding, a world with sense and meaning. Nothing showed me more clearly the passage from a perceptual to a conceptual world, a passage impossible without complex dialogue—a dialogue that first occurs with the parents, but is then internalized as "talking to oneself," as thought.

Dialogue launches language, the mind, but once it is launched we develop a new power, "inner speech," and it is this that is indispensable for our further development, our thinking. "Inner speech," says Vygotsky, "is speech almost without words . . . it is not the interior aspect of external speech, it is a function in itself. . . . While in external speech thought is embodied in words, in inner speech words die as they bring forth thought. Inner speech is to a large extent thinking in pure meanings." We start with dialogue, with language that is external and social, but then to think, to become ourselves, we have to move to a monologue, to inner speech. Inner speech is essentially solitary, and it is profoundly mysterious, as unknown to science, Vygotsky writes, as "the other side of the moon." "We are our language," it is often said; but our real language, our real identity, lies in inner speech, in that ceaseless stream and generation of meaning that constitutes the individual mind. It is through inner speech that the child develops his own concepts and meanings; it is through inner speech that he achieves his own identity; it is through inner speech, finally, that he constructs his own world. And the inner speech (or inner Sign) of the deaf may be very distinctive.[26]

It is evident to her parents that Charlotte constructs her world in a different way, perhaps radically so: that she employs predominantly visual thought patterns, and that she "thinks differently" about physical objects. I was struck by the graphic quality, the fullness of her descriptions. Her parents spoke too of this fullness: "All the characters or creatures or objects Charlotte talks about are *placed*," her mother said; "spatial reference is essential to ASL. When Charlotte signs, the whole scene is set up; you can see where everyone or everything is; it is all visualized with a detail that would be rare for the hearing." This placing of objects and people in specific locations, this use of elaborate, spatial reference had been striking in Charlotte, her parents said, since the age of four and a half—already at that age she had gone beyond them, shown a sort of "staging" power, an "architectural" power that they had seen in other deaf people—but rarely in the hearing.[27]

Language and thought, for us, are always personal—our utterances express ourselves, as does our inner speech. Language often feels to us, therefore, like an effusion, a sort of spontaneous transmission of self. It does not occur to us at first that it must have a *structure*, a structure of an immensely intricate and formal kind. We are unconscious of this structure; we do not see it, any more than we see the tissues, the organs, the architectural makeup of our own bodies. But the enormous, unique freedom of language would not be possible without the most extreme grammatical constraints. It is grammar, first of all, that makes a language possible, that allows us to articulate our thoughts, our selves, in utterance.

This was clear, in regard to speech, by 1660 (the date of the Port-Royal *Grammar*), but was only established, in regard to Sign, in 1960.[28] Sign was not seen, even by signers, as a true language, with its own grammar, before then. And yet the notion that Sign might have an internal structure is not entirely new—it has, so to speak, an odd prehistory of its own. Thus Roch-Ambroise Bébian, Sicard's successor, not only realized that Sign had an autonomous grammar of its own (and thus had no need of an alien and imported French grammar), but tried to compile a "Mimography" based on "The Decomposition of Signs." This enterprise failed, and had to fail, because there was no correct identification of the actual ("phonemic") elements of Sign.

In the 1870s E. B. Tylor, the anthropologist, had a deep interest in language, and this included a deep interest in and knowledge of Sign (he was a fluent signer, with many deaf friends).

His *Researches into the Early History of Mankind* contained many fascinating insights into signed language, and might have inaugurated a true linguistic study of Sign, had this enterprise not been killed, as was any just valuation of Sign, by the Milan conference of 1880. With the official and formal devaluation of Sign, linguists turned their attention elsewhere, and either ignored it, or misunderstood it completely. J. G. Kyle and B. Woll detail this sad history in their book, remarking that such was Tylor's knowledge of the grammar of Sign as to make it obvious that "linguists have only been *re*discovering [it] over the past ten years." Notions that "the sign language" of the deaf is no more than a sort of pantomime, or pictorial language, were almost universally held even thirty years ago. The *Encyclopedia Britannica* (14th ed.) calls it "a species of picture writing in the air"; and a well-known standard text tells us:[29]

The manual sign language used by the deaf is an Ideographic Language. Essentially it is more pictorial, less symbolic, and as a system is one which falls mainly at the level of imagery. Ideographic language systems, in comparison with verbal symbol systems, lack precision, subtlety and flexibility. It is likely that Man cannot achieve his ultimate potential through an Ideographic language, inasmuch as it is limited to the more concrete aspects of his experience.

There is, indeed, a paradox here: at first Sign looks pantomimic; if one pays attention, one feels, one will "get it" soon enough—all pantomimes are easy to get. But as one continues to look, no such "Aha!" feeling occurs; one is tantalized by finding it, despite its seeming transparency, unintelligible.[30]

There was no linguistic attention, no scientific attention,

given to Sign until the late 1950s when William Stokoe, a young medievalist and linguist, found his way to Gallaudet College. Stokoe thought he had come to teach Chaucer to the deaf; but he very soon perceived that he had been thrown, by good fortune or chance, into one of the world's most extraordinary linguistic environments. Sign language, at this time, was not seen as a proper language, but as a sort of pantomime or gestural code, or perhaps a sort of broken English on the hands. It was Stokoe's genius to see, and prove, that it was nothing of the sort; that it satisfied every linguistic criterion of a genuine language, in its lexicon and syntax, its capacity to generate an infinite number of propositions. In 1960 Stokoe published *Sign Language Structure*, and in 1965 (with his deaf colleagues Dorothy Casterline and Carl Croneberg) *A Dictionary of American Sign Language*. Stokoe was convinced that signs were *not* pictures, but complex abstract symbols with a complex inner structure. He was the first, then, to look for a structure, to analyze signs, to dissect them, to search for constituent parts. Very early he proposed that each sign had at least three independent parts—location, handshape, and movement (analogous to the phonemes of speech)—and that each part had a limited number of combinations.[31] In *Sign Language Structure* he delineated nineteen different handshapes, twelve locations, twenty-four types of movements, and invented a notation for these—American Sign Language had never been *written* before.[32] His *Dictionary* was equally original, for the signs were arranged not thematically (e.g., signs for food, signs for animals, etc.) but systematically, according to their parts, and organization, and principles of the language. It showed the lexical structure of the language—the linguistic interrelatedness of a basic three thousand sign "words."

It required a quiet and immense self-confidence, even obstinacy, to pursue these studies, for almost everyone, hearing and deaf alike, at first regarded Stokoe's notions as absurd or heretical; his books, when they came out, as worthless or nonsensical.[33] This is often the way with works of genius. But within a very few years, because of Stokoe's works, the entire climate of opinion had been changed, and a revolution—a double revolution—was under way: a scientific revolution, paying attention to sign language, and its cognitive and neural substrates, as no one had ever thought to do before; and a cultural and political revolution.

The *Dictionary of American Sign Language* listed three thousand root signs—which might seem to be an extremely limited vocabulary (compared, for instance, with the 600,000 words or so in the *Oxford English Dictionary*). And yet, manifestly, Sign is highly expressive, can express essentially anything that a spoken language can.[34] Clearly other, additional principles are at work. The great investigator of these other principles—of all that can turn a lexicon into a language—has been Ursula Bellugi and her collaborators at the Salk Institute.

A lexicon embodies all sorts of concepts, but these remain isolated (at the level of "Me Tarzan, you Jane") in the absence of a grammar. There has to be a formal system of rules, by which coherent utterances—sentences, propositions—can be generated. (This is not entirely obvious, an intuitive concept, for utterance itself seems so immediate, so seamless, so personal that one might not at first feel it contained, or required, a formal system of rules: this, surely, is one reason why it was native signers, above all, who felt their own language as "undecomposable," and regarded Stokoe's—and later, Bellugi's—efforts with incredulity.)

The idea of such a formal system, a "generative grammar," is itself not new. Humboldt spoke of every language as making "infinite use of finite means." But it is only in the last thirty years that we have been given, by Noam Chomsky, an explicit account of "how these finite means are put to infinite use in particular languages"—and an exploration of "the deeper properties that define 'human language' in general." These deeper properties Chomsky calls the "deep structure" of grammar; he sees them as an innate, species-specific characteristic in man, one that is latent in the nervous system until kindled by actual language use. Chomsky visualizes this "deep grammar" as consisting of a vast system of rules ("many hundreds of rules of different types"), containing a certain fixed general structure, which at times he sees as analogous to the visual cortex, which has all sorts of innate devices for ordering visual perception.[35] We are, as yet, almost totally ignorant of the neural substrate for such a grammar—but that there is one, and its approximate location, is indicated by the fact that there are aphasias, including Sign aphasias, in which grammatical competence, and this only, is specifically impaired.[36]

A person who knows a specific language, in Chomsky's formulation, is one who has control of "a grammar that *generates* . . . the infinite set of potential deep structures, maps them onto associated surface structures, and determines the semantic and phonetic interpretations of these abstract objects."[37] How does he get (or get control of) such a grammar? How can such a device be acquired by a two-year-old? A child who is certainly not taught grammar explicitly, and who is subject not to exemplary utterances—pieces of grammar—but to the most spontaneous, offhand (and seemingly uninformative) talk of his parents? (Of course, the language of the parents is not "uninformative," but full of implicit grammar and innumerable, unconscious linguistic hints and adjustments to which the child unconsciously responds. But there is no conscious or explicit transmission of grammar.) It is this which so strikes Chomsky—how the child is able to arrive at so much from so little.[38]

> We cannot avoid being struck by the enormous disparity between knowledge and experience, in the case of language, between the generative grammar that expresses the linguistic competence of the native speaker and the meager and degenerate data [to which he is exposed] on the basis of which he has constructed this grammar for himself.

The child, then, is not taught grammar; nor does he learn it; he *constructs* it from the "meager and degenerate data" at his disposal. And this would not be possible were the grammar, or its possibility, not already within him, in some latent form that is waiting to be actualized. There must be, as Chomsky puts it, "an innate structure that is rich enough to account for the disparity between experience and knowledge."

This innate structure, this latent structure, is not fully developed at birth, nor is it too obvious at the age of eighteen months. But then, suddenly, and in the most dramatic way, the developing child becomes open to language, becomes able to construct a grammar from the utterances of his parents. He shows a spectacular ability, a genius for language, between the ages of twenty-one and thirty-six months (this period is the same in all neurologically normal human beings, deaf as well as hearing; it is somewhat delayed, along with other developmental landmarks, in the retarded), and then a diminishing capacity, which ends at childhood's end (roughly at the age of twelve or thirteen).[39] This is, in Lenneberg's term, the "critical period" for acquiring a first language—the only period when the brain, from scratch, can actualize a complete grammar. The parents play an essential, but only facilitating, role here: language itself develops "from within" at the critical time, and all they do (in Humboldt's words) is "provide the thread along which it will develop of its own accord." The process is more like maturation than learning—the innate structure (which Chomsky sometimes calls a Language Acquisition Device, or LAD) grows organically, differentiates, matures, like an embryo.

Bellugi, speaking of her early works with Roger Brown, singles out the sense of this as constituting, for her, the central wonder of language; she refers to a joint paper describing the process of "induction of the latent structure" of sentences by the child, and its final sentence: "The very intricate simultaneous differentiation and integration that constitutes the evolution of the noun-phrase is more reminiscent of the biological development of an embryo than it is of the acquisition of a conditioned reflex." The *second* wonder of her life as a linguist, she says, was to see that this marvelous organic structure—the intricate embryo of grammar—could exist in a purely visual form, and that it did so in Sign.

Bellugi has, above all, studied the morphological processes of ASL—the ways in which a sign is changed to express different meanings through grammar and syntax. It was evident that the bare lexicon of the *Dictionary of American Sign* was only a first step—for a language is not just a lexicon or code. (Indian sign language, so-called, is a mere code—i.e., a collection or vocabulary of signs, the signs themselves having no internal structure and scarcely capable of being modified grammatically.) A genuine language is continually modulated by grammatical and syntactic devices of all sorts. There is an extraordinary richness of such devices in ASL, which serve to simplify the basic vocabulary hugely.

Thus there are numerous forms of LOOK-AT ("look-at-me," "look-at-her," "look-at-each-of-them," etc.), all of which are formed in distinctive ways: for example, the sign LOOK-AT is made with one hand moving away from the signer; but when inflected to mean "look at each other" is made with both hands moving towards each other simultaneously. A remarkable number of inflections are available to denote durational aspects (fig. 1); thus LOOK-AT (a) may be inflected to mean "stare" (b), "look at incessantly" (c), "gaze" (d), "watch" (e), "look for a long time" (f), or "look again and again" (g)—and many other permutations, including combinations of the above. Then there are large numbers of derivational forms, the sign LOOK being varied in specific ways to mean "reminisce," "sightsee," "look forward to," "prophesy," "predict," "anticipate," "look around aimlessly," "browse," etc.

The face may also serve special, linguistic functions in Sign: thus (as Corina, Liddell, and others have shown) specific facial expressions, or, rather "behaviors," may serve to mark syntactic constructions such as topics, relative clauses, and questions, or function as adverbs or quantifiers.[40] Other parts of the body may also be involved. Any or all of this—this vast range of actual or potential inflections, spatial and kinetic—can converge upon the root signs, fuse with them, and modify them, compacting an enormous amount of information into the resulting signs.

(a) Look at

(b) Stare

(c) Look at incessantly

(d) Gaze

(e) Watch

(f) Look for a long time

(g) Look again and again

Figure 1. The root sign LOOK-AT may be modified in many ways. These are some of the inflections for the temporal aspects of LOOK-AT; there are many others, for distinctions of degree, manner, number, etc. (Reprinted by permission [with change in notation] from *The Signs of Language*, E. S. Klima & U. Bellugi. Harvard University Press, 1979.)

It is the *compression* of these sign units, and the fact that all their modifications are *spatial*, that makes Sign, at the obvious and visible level, completely unlike any spoken language, and which, in part, prevented it from being seen as a language at all. But it is precisely this, along with its unique spatial syntax and grammar, which marks Sign as a true language—albeit a completely novel one, out of the evolutionary mainstream of all spoken languages, a unique evolutionary alternative. (And, in a way, a completely surprising one, considering we have become specialized for speech in the last half million or two million years. The potentials for language are in us all—this is easy to understand. But that the potentials for a *visual* language mode should also be so great—this is astonishing, and would hardly be anticipated if visual language did not actually occur. But, equally, it might be said that making signs and gestures, albeit without complex linguistic structure, goes back to our remote, prehuman past—and that speech is really the evolutionary newcomer; a highly successful newcomer which could replace the hands, freeing them for other, non-communicational purposes. Perhaps, indeed, there have been two parallel evolutionary streams for spoken and signed forms of language: this is suggested by the work of certain anthropologists, who have shown the co-existence of spoken and signed languages in some primitive tribes.[41] Thus the deaf, and their language, show us not only the plasticity but the latent potentials of the nervous system.)

The single most remarkable feature of Sign—that which distinguishes it from all other languages and mental activities—is its unique linguistic use of space.[42] The complexity of this linguistic space is quite overwhelming for the "normal" eye, which cannot see, let alone understand, the sheer intricacy of its spatial patterns.

We see then, in Sign, at every level—lexical, grammatical, syntactic—a *linguistic* use of space: a use that is amazingly complex, for much of what occurs linearly, sequentially, temporally in speech, becomes simultaneous, concurrent, multileveled in Sign. The "surface" of Sign may appear simple to the eye, like that of gesture or mime, but one soon finds that this is an illusion, and what looks so simple is extraordinarily complex and consists of innumerable spatial patterns nested, three-dimensionally, in each other.[43]

The marvel of this spatial grammar, of the linguistic use of space, engrossed Sign researchers in the 1970s, and it is only in the present decade that equal attention has been paid to time. Although it was recognized earlier that there was sequential organization within signs, this was regarded as phonologically unimportant, basically because it could not be "read." It has required the insights of a new generation of linguists—linguists who are themselves often deaf, or native users of Sign, who can analyze its refinements from their own experience of it, from "within"—to bring out the importance of such sequences within (and between) signs. The Supalla brothers, Ted and Sam, among others, have been pioneers here. Thus, in a groundbreaking 1978 paper, Ted Supalla and Elissa Newport demonstrated that very finely detailed differences in movement could distinguish some nouns from related verbs: it had been thought earlier (for example, by Stokoe) that there was a single sign for "sit" and "chair"—but Supalla and Newport showed the signs for these were subtly but crucially separate.

The most systematic research on the use of time in Sign has been done by Scott Liddell and Robert Johnson and their colleagues at Gallaudet. Liddell and Johnson see signing not as a succession of instantaneous "frozen" configurations in space, but as continually and richly modulated in time, with a dynamism of "movements" and "holds" analogous to that of music or speech. They have demonstrated many types of sequentiality in ASL signing—sequences of handshapes, locations, non-manual signs, local movements, movements-and-holds—as well as internal (phonological) segmentation within signs. The simultaneous model of structure is not able to represent such sequences, and may indeed prevent their being seen. Thus it has been necessary to replace the older static notions and descriptions with new, and often very elaborate, dynamic notations, which have some resemblances to the notations for dance and music.[44]

No one has watched these new developments with more interest than Stokoe himself, and he has focused specifically on the powers of "language in four dimensions":[45]

> Speech has only one dimension—its extension in time; writing has two dimensions; models have three; but only signed languages have at their disposal four dimensions—the three spatial dimensions accessible to a signer's body, as well as the dimension of time. And Sign fully exploits the syntactic possibilities in its four-dimensional channel of expression.

The effect of this, Stokoe feels—and here he is supported by the intuitions of Sign artists, playwrights, and actors—is that signed language is not merely proselike and narrative in structure, but essentially "cinematic" too:

> In a signed language . . . narrative is no longer linear and prosaic. Instead, the essence of sign language is to cut from a normal view to a close-up to a distant shot to a close-up again, and so on, even including flashback and flash-forward scenes,

exactly as a movie editor works. . . . Not only is signing itself arranged more like edited film than like written narration, but also each signer is placed very much as a camera: the field of vision and angle of view are directed but variable. Not only the signer signing but also the signer watching is aware at all times of the signer's visual orientation to what is being signed about.

Thus, in this third decade of research, Sign is seen as fully comparable to speech (in terms of its phonology, its temporal aspects, its streams and sequences), but with unique, additional powers of a spatial and cinematic sort—at once a most complex and yet transparent expression and transformation of thought.[46]

The cracking of this enormously complex, four-dimensional structure may need the most formidable hardware, as well as an insight approaching genius.[47] And yet it can also be cracked, effortlessly, unconsciously, by a three-year-old signer.[48]

What goes on in the mind and brain of a three-year-old signer, or any signer, that makes him such a genius at Sign, makes him able to use space, to "linguisticize" space, in this astonishing way? What sort of hardware does *he* have in his head? One would not think, from the "normal" experience of speech and speaking, or from the neurologist's understanding of speech and speaking, that such spatial virtuosity could occur. It may indeed not be possible for the "normal" brain—i.e., the brain of someone who has not been exposed early to Sign.[49] What then is the neurological basis of Sign?

Having spent the 1970s exploring the structure of sign languages, Ursula Bellugi and her colleagues are now examining its neural substrates. This involves, among other methods, the classical method of neurology, which is to analyze the effects

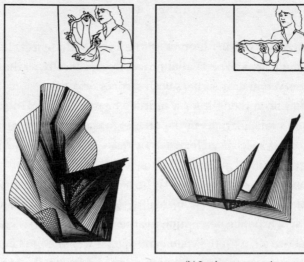

(a) Look all over

(b) Look across a series

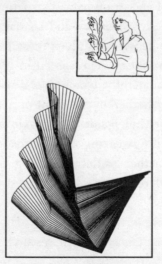

(c) Look at internal features

Figure 2. Computer-generated images showing three different grammatical inflections of the sign LOOK. The beauty of a spatial grammar, with its complex three-dimensional trajectories, is well brought out by this technique. (Reprinted by permission from Ursula Bellugi. The Salk Institute for Biological Studies, La Jolla, California.)

produced by various lesions of the brain—the effect, here, on
sign language and on spatial processing generally, as these may
be observed in deaf signers with strokes or other lesions.

It has been thought for a century or more (since Hughlings-
Jackson's formulations in the 1870s) that the left hemisphere of
the brain is specialized for analytic tasks, above all for the lexical
and grammatical analysis that makes the understanding of spoken language possible. The right hemisphere has been seen as
complementary in function, dealing in wholes rather than parts,
with synchronous perceptions rather than sequential analyses,
and, above all, with the visual and spatial world. Sign languages
clearly cut across these neat boundaries—for on the one hand,
they have lexical and grammatical structure, but on the other,
this structure is synchronous and spatial. Thus it was quite
uncertain even a decade ago, given these peculiarities, whether
sign language would be represented in the brain unilaterally
(like speech) or bilaterally; which side, if unilateral, it would be
represented on; whether, in the event of a sign aphasia, syntax
might be disturbed independently of lexicon; and, most intriguingly, given the interweaving of grammatical and spatial relations in Sign, whether spatial processing, overall spatial sense,
might have a different (and conceivably stronger) neural basis
in deaf signers.[50]

These were some of the questions faced by Bellugi and her colleagues when they launched their research. At the time, actual
reports on the effects of strokes and other brain lesions on signing were rare, unclear, and often inadequately studied—in part
because there was little differentiation between finger spelling
and Sign. Indeed, Bellugi's first and central finding was that the
left hemisphere of the brain *is* essential for Sign, as it is for
speech, that Sign uses some of the same neural pathways as are

needed for the processing of grammatical speech—but in addition, some pathways normally associated with visual processing.

That signing uses the left hemisphere predominantly has also been shown by Helen Neville, who has demonstrated that Sign is "read" more rapidly and accurately by signers when it is presented in the right visual field (information from each side of the visual field is always processed in the opposite hemisphere). This may also be shown, in the most dramatic way, by observing the effects of lesions (from strokes, etc.) in certain areas of the left hemisphere. Such lesions may cause an aphasia for Sign—a breakdown in the understanding or use of Sign analogous to the aphasias of speech. Such sign aphasias can affect either the lexicon or the grammar (including the spatially organized syntax) of Sign differentially, as well as impairing the general power to "propositionize" which Hughlings-Jackson saw as central to language.[51] But aphasic signers are *not* impaired in other, nonlinguistic visual-spatial abilities. (Gesture, for example— the nongrammatical expressive movements we all make [shrugging the shoulders, waving good-bye, brandishing a fist, etc.]—is preserved in aphasia, even though Sign is lost, emphasizing the absolute distinction between the two. Patients with aphasia, indeed, can be taught to use "Amerindian Gestural Code," but cannot use Sign, any more than they can use speech.)[52] Signers with right hemisphere strokes, in contrast, may have severe spatial disorganization, an inability to appreciate perspective, and sometimes neglect of the left side of space—but are not aphasic and retain perfect signing ability despite their severe visual-spatial deficits. Thus signers show the same cerebral lateralization as speakers, even though their language is entirely visuospatial in nature (and as such might be expected to be processed in the right hemisphere).

This finding, when one considers it, is both startling and obvious and leads to two conclusions. It confirms, at a neurological level, that Sign *is* a language and is treated as such by the brain, even though it is visual rather than auditory, and spatially rather than sequentially organized. And as a language, it is processed by the left hemisphere of the brain, which is biologically specialized for just this function.

The fact that Sign is based here in the left hemisphere, despite its spatial organization, suggests that there is a representation of "linguistic" space in the brain completely different from that of ordinary, "topographic" space. Bellugi provides a remarkable and startling confirmation of this. One of her subjects, Brenda I., with a massive right hemisphere lesion, showed a profound neglect of the left side of space, so that when she described her room, she put everything, higgledy-piggledy, on the right side, leaving the left side entirely vacant. The left side of space—of topographic space—no longer existed for her (fig. 3a–b). But in the actual signing, she established spatial loci, and signed freely, throughout the signing space, including the left side (fig. 3c). Thus her perceptual space, her topographic space, a right hemisphere function, was profoundly defective; but her linguistic space, her syntax space, a left hemisphere function, was completely intact.

Thus there develops in signers a new and extraordinarily sophisticated way of representing space; a new *sort* of space, a formal space, which has no analogue in those of us who do not sign.[53] This reflects a wholly novel neurological development. It is as if the left hemisphere in signers "takes over" a realm of visual-spatial perception, modifies it, sharpens it, in an unprecedented way, giving it a new, highly analytical and abstract character, making a visual language and visual conception possible.[54]

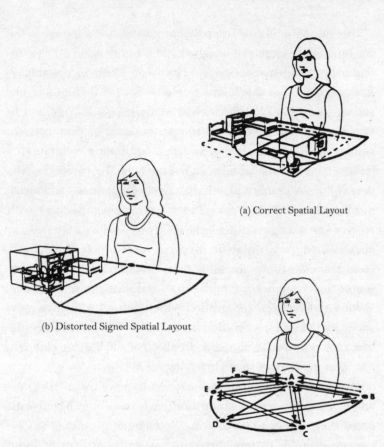

(a) Correct Spatial Layout

(b) Distorted Signed Spatial Layout

(c) Correct Signed Syntax

Figure 3. A massive lesion in the right cerebral hemisphere destroys Brenda I.'s ability to "map" on the left side, but not her ability to use syntax. Figure (a) shows the actual layout of Brenda's room, as it would be correctly signed. Figure (b): In describing her room, Brenda leaves the left side bare, and (mentally) piles all the furniture in the right side of the room. She can no longer even imagine "leftness." Figure (c): But in her actual signing, Brenda uses a full space, including the left side, to represent syntactic relations. (Reprinted by permission from *What the Hands Reveal About the Brain*, H. Poizner, E. S. Klima, & U. Bellugi. The MIT Press/Bradford Books, 1987.)

One must wonder whether this linguistic-spatial power is the only special development in signers. Do they develop other, non-linguistic, visual-spatial powers? Does a new form of visual *intelligence* become possible? This question has led Bellugi and her colleagues to launch a fascinating study of visual cognition in deaf signers. They compared the performance of deaf, natively signing children with that of hearing, nonsigning children on a battery of visual-spatial tests. In tests of spatial construction, the deaf children did much better than the hearing ones, and indeed, much better than "normal." There were similar findings with tests of spatial organization—the ability to perceive a whole from disorganized parts, the ability to perceive (or conceive) an object. Here again, deaf four-year-olds did extraordinarily well, getting scores that some hearing high school students could not match. With a test of facial recognition—the Benton test, which measures both facial recognition and spatial transformation—the deaf children were again markedly ahead of the hearing children, and far in advance of their chronological norms.

Perhaps the most dramatic test results have come from deaf and hearing children in Hong Kong, where Bellugi has investigated their ability to perceive and remember meaningless Chinese "pseudo-characters" presented as swift patterns of light. Here the deaf, signing children did startlingly well—and the hearing children were almost unable to do the task at all (see fig. 4). The deaf children, it seems, were able to "parse" these pseudo-characters, to achieve a very complex spatial analysis, and this enormously facilitated their powers of visual perception, enabling them to "see" the pseudo-characters at a glance. Even when the experiment was repeated with deaf and hearing American adults who had no knowledge of Chinese characters, the deaf signers did notably better.

Target Structure Point Light Motion

Deaf Chinese Children

Hearing Chinese Children

Figure 4. Asked to reproduce a Chinese pseudo-character (presented as a moving point light display), deaf Chinese children do extremely well, and hearing Chinese children extremely badly. (Reprinted by permission from "Dyslexia: Perspectives from Sign and Script," U. Bellugi, Q. Tzeng, E. S. Klima, and A. Fok. In *From Reading to Neurons*, A. Galaburda, ed., The MIT Press/Bradford Press, 1989.)

These tests, in which signing children perform far above normal levels (a superiority that is especially marked in the first few years of life), all emphasize the special visual skills learned in acquiring Sign. As Bellugi notes, the spatial organization test involves not only the recognition and naming of objects, but also mental rotation, form perception, and spatial organization, all of which are relevant to the spatial underpinnings of Sign syntax. The ability to discriminate faces, and recognize subtle variations of facial expression, also carries extreme importance to the signer, since facial expression plays an important role in ASL grammar.[55]

The ability to separate discrete configurations, or "frames," from a continuous stream of movement (as was done with the Chinese pseudo-characters) brings out another important ability of signers—their enhanced power of "movement parsing." This is seen as being analogous to the ability to break down and analyze speech from a continuous and ever-changing pattern of sound waves. All of us have this ability in the auditory sphere—but only signers have it so dramatically in the visual sphere. And this too, of course, is essential to the comprehension of a visual language, which is extended in time as well as in space.

Is it possible to detect a cerebral basis for such enhancement of spatial cognition? Neville has studied the physiological correlates for such perceptual changes, by measuring changes in the brain's electrical responses (evoked potentials) to visual stimuli in particular, movements in the peripheral visual field. (Enhanced perception of such stimuli is crucial in Sign communication, for the signer's eyes are generally fixed on the other's face, and signing movements of the hands therefore lie in the periphery of the visual field.) She has compared these responses in three groups of subjects: deaf native signers, hearing non-signers, and hearing native signers (usually born of deaf parents).

Deaf signers show greater speed of reaction to these stimuli—and this goes with an increase of evoked potentials in the occipital lobes of the brain, the primary reception areas for vision. Such increases of speed and occipital potentials were not observed in any of the hearing subjects, and seem to reflect a compensatory phenomenon—the enhancement of one sense in place of another (greater auditory sensitivities, similarly, may occur in the blind).[56]

But there were also enhancements at higher levels: the deaf subjects showed greater accuracy in detecting the direction of motion, especially when the movement was in the right visual field, and coincident with this was an increase in evoked potentials in the parietal regions of the left hemisphere. These enhancements were also observed in the hearing children of deaf parents and have therefore to be seen not as an effect of deafness, but as an effect of the early acquisition of Sign (which demands very superior perception of visual stimuli). It is not only detection of motion in the peripheral field that is shifted, in signers, from being a right hemisphere to a left hemisphere function. Neville and Bellugi obtained evidence—indeed, quite early on—for a similar left hemisphere specialization (and shift from the "normal" right hemisphere specialization) in deaf signers for picture identification, dot localization, and the recognition of faces.[57]

But the very greatest enhancements were observed in deaf signers—and in these, intriguingly, the enhancement of evoked potentials spread forward into the left temporal lobe, which is normally regarded as purely auditory in function. This is a very remarkable and, one suspects, fundamental finding, for it suggests that what are normally auditory areas are being *reallo-cated*, in deaf signers, for visual processing. It constitutes one of the most astonishing demonstrations of the plasticity of the nervous system, and the extent of its adaptability to a different sensory mode.[58]

Such a finding also raises fundamental questions as to the extent to which the nervous system, or at least the cerebral cortex, is fixed by inborn genetic constraints (with fixed centers and fixed localization—areas "hardwired," "preprogrammed," or "prededicated" for specific functions) and to what extent it is plastic and may be modified by the particularities of sensory experience. The famous experiments of Hubel and Wiesel have shown how greatly the visual cortex may be modified by visual stimuli, but leave unclear how much input merely kindles built-in potentials, and how much it actually shapes and molds them. The experiments of Neville suggest a shaping of function to experience—for it can hardly be supposed that the auditory cortex has been "waiting" for deafness, or visual stimulation, to become visual and change its character. It is very difficult to explain such findings except by a radically different sort of theory, one that does not see the nervous system as a universal machine, hardwired and preprogrammed for (potentially) everything, but sees it as *becoming* different, as free to take on completely different forms, within the constraints of what is genetically possible.

To comprehend the significance of these findings one also needs a different way of looking at the cerebral hemispheres and their differences and their dynamic roles in dealing with cognitive tasks. Such a way has been provided by Elkhonon

Goldberg and his colleagues in a series of experimental and theoretical papers.

Classically the two cerebral hemispheres are seen as having fixed (or "committed") and mutually exclusive functions: linguistic/nonlinguistic, sequential/simultaneous, and analytic/gestalt are among the dichotomies suggested. This view runs into obvious difficulties when one confronts a visuospatial language.

Goldberg would first enlarge the domain of "language" to one of "descriptive systems" in general. Such descriptive systems, in his formulation, constitute superstructures imposed on elementary "feature detection" systems (for example, those of the visual cortex), a variety of such systems (or "codes") being operative in normal cognition. One such system is, of course, natural language; but there may be many others—such as formal mathematical languages, musical notation, games, etc. (insofar as these are encoded by special notations). It is characteristic of all of these that they are first approached in a tentative, groping way but later acquire an automatic perfection. Thus there may be with these, and with all cognitive tasks, two ways of approach, two cerebral "strategies," and a shift (with the acquisition of skill) from one to the other. The right hemisphere's role, as thus conceived, is critical for dealing with *novel* situations, for which there does not yet exist any established descriptive system or code—and it is also seen as playing a part in assembling such codes. Once such a code has been assembled, or emerged, there is a transfer of function from right to left hemisphere, for the latter controls all processes that are organized in terms of such grammars or codes. (Thus a novel linguistic task, even though it is linguistic, will initially be processed predominantly by the right hemisphere, and only subsequently become routinized as a left hemisphere function. And a visuospatial task, conversely, even though it is visuospatial, will, if it can be embedded in a notation or code, come to show a left hemisphere superiority.)[59]

With such an approach—so different from the classical doctrines of fixed hemispheral specificities—one can understand the role of the *individual's* experience and his development, as he moves from his first gropings (in linguistic or other cognitive tasks) toward expertise and perfection.[60] (Neither hemisphere is "more advanced" or "better" than the other; they are merely suited for different dimensions and stages of processing. Both are complementary, interacting; and between them they allow the mastery of new tasks.) Such a view makes clear, without paradox, how Sign (though visuospatial) can become a left hemisphere function, and how many other sorts of visual ability—from perception of movement to perception of patterns, perception of spatial relation to perception of facial expressions—by having become part of signing, will be swept along with it, as it develops, into becoming left hemisphere functions too. We can understand why the signer becomes a sort of visual "expert" in many ways, in certain nonlinguistic as well as linguistic tasks—how there may develop not just visual language but a special visual sensibility and intelligence as well.

We need more hard evidence about the development of a "higher" visuality, a visual style, comparable to the evidence Bellugi and Neville have provided about the enhancement of "lower" visual-cognitive functions in the deaf.[61] As yet we have mostly anecdotes and accounts; but the accounts are extraordinary and demand close attention. Even Bellugi and her colleagues, who rarely depart from rigorously scientific description, are moved to include the following brief account, in passing, in their book, *What the Hands Reveal About the Brain.*[62]

> We first saw this mapping aspect of signing in its full form
> when a visiting deaf friend was telling us about his recent
> move to new quarters. For five minutes or so, he described the
> garden cottage in which he now lived—rooms, layout, furni-
> ture, windows, landscaping and so forth. He described it in
> exquisite detail, and with such explicit signing that we felt he
> had sculpted the entire cottage, garden, hills, trees and all in
> front of us.

What is related here is difficult (for the rest of us) to imagine—it has to be seen. It is very similar to what Charlotte's parents say of her—her ability to create a real (or fictional)
landscape with such precision, such fullness, such aliveness, as
to transport the beholder. The use of such picturing, pictorial
power, goes with the use of Sign—even though Sign is not in
the least a "picture-language" itself.

The other side of this linguistic expertise, and visual expertise generally, is the tragically poor linguistic and intellectual
function that may afflict a large number of deaf children. It is
clear that the high linguistic and visual competences of the
well-functioning deaf lead to the establishment of strong cerebral lateralization, with a shift of language functions (and also
visual-cognitive functions generally) to a well-developed *left*
hemisphere. But what, we have to wonder, is the situation, neurologically, with the poorly functioning deaf?

Rapin was struck by "a remarkable linguistic deficiency" in
many of the deaf children she works with—specifically, an
inability to understand question forms, to understand the struc-

ture of sentences—an inability to manipulate the language-code. Schlesinger shows us other dimensions of this deficiency, dimensions that expand it from the linguistic to the intellectual: the low-functioning deaf, in her description, not only have difficulty in the understanding of questions, but refer only to objects in the immediate environment, do not conceive remoteness or contingencies, do not formulate hypotheses, do not rise to superordinate categories, and are in general confined to a preconceptual, perceptual world. She feels that their utterances are somewhat deficient syntactically and semantically, but clearly are also deficient in a much deeper sense.

How then should we characterize their deficiency? We need another kind of characterization, one that transcends the usual linguistic categories of syntax, semantics, phonetics. Such a characterization has again been provided by Goldberg in his reflections on "isolated right hemisphere speech." Right hemisphere language allows *ad hoc* referential relations (pointing to, labeling, this-here-now)—the establishing of a referential basis of a linguistic code—but cannot go beyond this to allow manipulations of the code, or internal derivations within it. In more general terms, right hemisphere functioning is restricted to perceptual organization and cannot shift to categorical, definition-based lexical organization; it is (in Zaidel's term) "experiential" only and cannot embrace the "paradigmatic."[63]

This referential processing, with complete absence of rule manipulation, is precisely what we see in deaf people who are linguistically defective. Their language, their lexical organization, is *like* that of people with right hemisphere speech. Such a condition is usually associated with left hemisphere damage, acquired in later life, but it could also arise as a mishap in development—as a failure to shift from an initial, right hemisphere, quasi-perceptual functioning to a mature, left hemisphere, fully linguistic functioning.

Is there any evidence that this does indeed occur in linguistically defective, low-functioning deaf people? Lenneberg questioned whether a large number of the congenitally deaf might have poorly established cerebral lateralization, though at the time (1967) there had not yet been any precise delineation of the differential lexical capacities and characters of the hemispheres in isolation. The matter has been approached, neurophysiologically, by Neville, who writes, "If language experience does impact cerebral development, then aspects of cerebral specialization ought to be different in deaf and hearing subjects when they read English." And indeed she finds that the majority of deaf people she tested do not show the pattern of left hemisphere specialization observed in the hearing. This, she hypothesizes, is because they lack full grammatical competence in English. And indeed, four congenitally deaf subjects of Neville's who had perfect English grammar showed "normal" left hemisphere specialization. Thus, in Neville's words, "grammatical competence is necessary and sufficient for left hemisphere specialization—if it occurs early."

It is clear from the phenomenological descriptions of Rapin and Schlesinger, and from the behavioral and neurophysiological evidence amassed by Neville, that language experience can grossly alter cerebral development—and that if it is severely deficient, or otherwise aberrant, it may delay the maturation of the brain, preventing proper left hemisphere development, in effect confining the person to a right hemisphere sort of language.[64]

It is not clear how long-lasting such delays may be; Schlesinger's observations suggest that, if not prevented, they may be lifelong. But they can be mitigated, and even reversed, by the right sort of intervention later, in adolescence.[65] Thus Braefield, a primary school, presents a horrifying picture but a few years later, as adolescents, the same students—or many of them—may be doing better, for example, at Lexington, a secondary school. (And, in quite a different mode from "intervention," there may be a belated discovery of the deaf world, and this can provide a linguistic intimacy and a culture and community, an at-long-last "coming home" that may compensate somewhat for earlier isolation.)

These, then, in very general terms, are the neurological hazards of congenital deafness. Neither language nor the higher forms of cerebral development occur "spontaneously"; they depend on exposure to language, communication, and proper language use. If deaf children are not exposed, early, to good language or communication, there may be a delay (even an arrest) of cerebral maturation, with a continuing predominance of right hemisphere processes and a lag in hemispheric "shift." But if language, a linguistic code, can be introduced by puberty, the form of the code (speech or Sign) does not seem to matter; it matters only that it be good enough to allow internal manipulation—then the normal shift to left hemisphere predominance can occur. And if the primary language is Sign, there will be, additionally, an enhancement of many sorts of visual-cognitive ability, all going along with a shift from right hemisphere to left hemisphere dominance.[66]

Very recently, there have been some fascinating observations with regard to the brain's disposition to sign language when it is exposed to it—in particular, its tendency toward ASL-like, or (in more general terms) Sign-like, forms *whatever* form of sign language it is exposed to. Thus James Paul Gee and Wendy Goodhart have shown dramatically that when deaf children are exposed to signed forms of English (manually encoded English), *but not ASL,* they "tend to innovate ASL-like forms with little or no input in that language." This is an astonishing finding: that a child who has never seen ASL nonetheless evolves ASL-like forms.

Elissa Newport and Ted Supalla have shown that children construct grammatically perfect ASL even when they are exposed (as they so often are) to somewhat less-than-perfect ASL—a clear illustration of an innate grammatical competence in the brain.[67] Gee and Goodhart's findings go further, by showing that the brain moves inevitably toward Sign-like forms, and will even "convert" non-Sign-like forms *to* Sign-like-forms. "Sign is closer to the language of the mind," as Edward Klima says, and thus more "natural" than anything else when the developing child is called upon to construct a language in the manual mode.

Sam Supalla has provided independent confirmation of these studies.[68] Focusing in particular on the sort of devices used to mark grammatical relations (these are all spatial in ASL, but in signed English, as in spoken English, entirely sequential), he has found that deaf children exposed only to signed English *replace* its grammatical devices with purely spatial ones "similar to those found in ASL or other natural signed languages." Supalla speaks of these as being "spontaneously created," or evolved.

It has been known for many years that signed English is cumbersome and imposes a strain on those who use it: "Deaf people," writes Bellugi, "have reported to us that while they can process each item as it appears, they find it difficult to process the message content as a whole when all the information is expressed in the sign stream as sequential elements." These difficulties, which do not diminish with use, are due to fundamental neurological limitations—in particular, of short-term memory and cognitive processing. None of these difficulties occurs with ASL, which with its spatial devices is perfectly adapted to a visual mode, and can be easily signed and understood at high speed. The overloading of short-term memory and cognitive capacity that occurs with signed English in deaf adults is experienced as difficulty and strain. But in deaf children, who still have the capacity to *create* grammatical structures—so Supalla hypothesizes—the cognitive difficulties involved in trying to learn signed speech force the children to create their own linguistic structures, to create or evolve a spatial grammar.

If deaf children are exposed only to signed English, Supalla has further shown, they may exhibit "impaired potential for natural language acquisition and processing," impairment of their capacity to create and comprehend grammar, unless they are able to create their own linguistic structures. Fortunately, being children, and still at a "Chomskian" age, they *are* able to create their own linguistic structures, their own spatial grammar. They resort to doing this in order to ensure their own linguistic survival.

These findings on the spontaneous origination of Sign, or Sign-like linguistic structures, in children may cast a very important light on the origin and evolution of Sign in general. For it appears as if the nervous system, given the constraints of language in a visual medium, and the physiological limitations of short-term memory and cognitive processing, *has* to evolve the sort of linguistic structures, the sort of spatial organization, we see in Sign. And there is strong circumstantial support for this in the fact that all indigenous signed languages—and there are many hundreds, all over the world, which have evolved separately and independently wherever there are groups of deaf people[69]—*all* indigenous signed languages have much the same spatial structure. None of them resembles signed English, or signed speech, in the least. All have, beneath their specific differences, some generic resemblance to ASL. There is no universal sign language, but there are, it seems, universals in all sign languages, universals not of meaning, but of grammatical form.[70]

There is good reason to suppose (though the evidence is circumstantial rather than direct) that general linguistic competence is genetically determined and is essentially the same in all human beings. But the particular form of grammar—what Chomsky calls "surface" grammar (whether this be the grammar of English or Chinese or Sign)—is determined by the experience of the individual; it is not a genetic endowment but an epigenetic achievement. It is "learned," or perhaps one should say, for we are dealing with something primitive and preconscious, it *evolves* through the interaction of a general (or abstract) linguistic competence and the particularities of experience—an experience which, in the deaf, is distinctive, indeed unique, because it is in a visual mode.

What Gee and Goodhart, and Samuel Supalla, observe *is* an evolution, a startling (and radical) modification of grammatical forms, under the influence of this visual necessity. They describe a change, a grammatical form changing visibly before the eyes, becoming spatialized, as signed English is "turned into" an ASL-like language. They depict an evolution of grammatical forms—but an evolution occurring within the course of a few months.

Language is actively modified, the brain itself is actively

modified, as it develops a wholly new capacity to "linguisticize" space (or to spatialize language). As the brain does this, it simultaneously develops all the other visual-cognitive, but non-linguistic, enhancements that Bellugi and Neville have described. There must be physiological and (could we but see them) anatomical shiftings and reorganizations in the micro-structure of the brain. Neville conceives the brain as having, at first, a great neuronal redundancy and plasticity, and of this being subsequently "pruned" by experience, here reinforcing synapses, connections between nerve cells, there inhibiting or suppressing them, according to the competing pressures of different sensory inputs. It is clear that genetic endowment alone cannot explain the full connectional complexity of the nervous system—whatever invariants are predetermined, additional diversity emerges during development. This postnatal development, or epigenesis, is the central concern of Jean-Pierre Changeux's work.

But a more radical suggestion, indeed a wholly different way of thinking, has recently been put forward by Gerald Edelman.[71] The unit of selection for Changeux is the individual neuron; the unit of selection for Edelman is the neuronal group, and it is only at this level, with selection of different neuronal groups or populations under competitive pressures, that *evolution* (as distinct from mere growth or development) may be said to occur. This allows Edelman to produce a model which is essentially biological, indeed Darwinian, in nature.[72] Darwin conceives of natural selection occurring in populations in response to environmental pressures. Edelman sees this as continuing *in the organism* (he speaks here of "somatic selection"), determining the individual development of the nervous system. The fact that *populations* of nerve cells, and not merely individual cells, are involved allows far more complex potentials for change.

Edelman's theory provides a detailed picture of how neuronal "maps" can be formed, which allow an animal to adapt (without innate programs or instruction) to wholly new perceptual challenges, to create or construct new perceptual forms and categorizations, new orientations, new approaches to the world. This is precisely the situation of the deaf child: he is flung into a perceptual (and cognitive and linguistic) situation for which there is neither genetic precedent nor teaching to assist him; and yet, given half a chance, he will develop radically new forms of neural organization, neural mappings, which will allow him to master the language-world, and articulate it, in a quite novel way. It is difficult to think of a more dramatic example of somatic selection, of neural Darwinism, in action.[73]

To be deaf, to be born deaf, places one in an extraordinary situation; it exposes one to a range of linguistic possibilities, and hence to a range of intellectual and cultural possibilities, which the rest of us, as native speakers in a world of speech, can scarcely even begin to imagine. We are neither deprived nor challenged, linguistically, as the deaf are: we are never in danger of languagelessness, or severe linguistic incompetence; but nor do we discover, or create, a startlingly new language.

The unspeakable experiment of King Psammetichos—who had two children raised by shepherds who never spoke to them, in order to see what (if any) language they would speak naturally— is repeated, potentially, with all children born deaf.[74] A small number—perhaps 10 percent of these—are born of deaf parents, exposed to Sign from the start, and become native signers. The rest must live in an aural-oral world, neither biologically, nor linguistically, nor emotionally well-equipped to deal with them. Deafness as such is not the affliction; affliction enters with the breakdown of communication and language. If communication cannot be achieved, if the child is not exposed to good language and dialogue, we see all the mishaps Schlesinger describes—mishaps at once linguistic, intellectual, emotional, and cultural. These mishaps are imposed, to a larger or smaller degree, upon the majority of those born deaf: "most deaf children," as Schein remarks, "grow up like strangers in their own households."[75]

Yet none of this has to happen. Although the dangers that threaten a deaf child are very great, they are, mercifully, entirely preventable. To be the parents of a deaf child, or of twins, or of a blind child, or of a prodigy, demands a special resilience and resourcefulness.[76] Many parents of the deaf feel powerless in the face of such a communication barrier with their child, and it is a tribute to the adaptability of both parents and child that this potentially devastating barrier can be overcome.

Finally, still too rarely, there are the deaf who fare well, at least in terms of realizing their innate capacities. Crucial to this is the acquisition of language at a "normal" early age—this first language can be Sign or speech (as we see with Charlotte and Alice), for it is *language*, rather than any particular language, that kindles linguistic competence and, with this, intellectual competence too. As the parents of deaf children have to be, in a sense, "super-parents," so deaf children themselves have to be, even more obviously, "super-children." Thus Charlotte is already, at six, a fluent reader, with a real and unforced passion for reading. She is already, at six, bilingual and bicultural—whereas most of us spend our whole lives in one language and one culture. Such differences can be positive and creative, can enrich human nature and culture. And this, if you will, is the other side of deafness—the special powers of visuality and Sign. The acquisition of Sign grammar occurs in much the same way, and at much the same age, as the grammar of speech—we may take it that the deep structure of both is identical. The propositional power of both is identical. The formal properties of both are identical, even though they involve, as Petitto and Bellugi say, different types of signals, different kinds of information, different sensory systems, different memory structures, and perhaps different neural structures. The formal properties of Sign and speech are identical, and so too is their communicational intent. Yet are they, or can they be, in some way, deeply different?

Chomsky reminds us that Humboldt "introduced a further distinction between the form of a language and what he calls its 'character' . . . [this latter being] determined by the way in which language is *used*, and thus to be distinguished from its syntactic and semantic structure, which are matters of form, not use." There is indeed a certain danger (as Humboldt pointed out) that in examining more and more deeply the form of a language, one may actually forget that it has a meaning, character, a use. Language is not just a formal device (though it is, indeed, the most marvelous of formal devices), but the most exact expression of our thoughts, our aspirations, our view of the world. The "character" of a language, as Humboldt speaks of it, is of an essentially creative and cultural nature, has a generic character, is its "spirit," not just its "style." English, in this sense, has a different character from German, and Shakespeare's language a different character from Goethe's. The cultural or personal identity is different. But Sign differs from speech more than any spoken language from another. Could there here be a radically different "organic" identity?

One has only to watch two people signing to see that signing has a playful quality, a style, quite different from that of speech. Signers tend to improvise, to play with signs, to bring all their humor, their imaginativeness, their personality, into their signing, so that signing is not just the manipulation of symbols according to grammatical rules, but, irreducibly, the voice of the signer—a voice given a special force, because it utters itself, so immediately, with the body. One can have or imagine disembodied speech, but one cannot have disembodied Sign. The body and soul of the signer, his unique human identity, are continually expressed in the act of signing.

Sign perhaps has a different origin from speech, since it arises from gesture, spontaneous emotional-motor representation.[77] And though Sign is fully formalized and grammaticized, it is highly iconic, it retains many traces of its representational origins. Deaf people, write Klima and Bellugi,

> are acutely aware of the undertones and overtones of iconicity in their vocabulary. . . . In communicating among themselves, or in narrative, deaf signers often extend, enhance, or exaggerate mimetic properties. Manipulation of the iconic aspect of signs also occurs in special heightened uses of language (Sign poetry and art Sign). . . . Thus ASL remains a two-faceted language—formally structured and yet in significant respects mimetically free.

While the formal properties, the deep structure, of Sign allow the most abstract concepts and propositions to be expressed, its iconic or mimetic aspect allows it to be extraordinarily concrete and evocative, in a way, perhaps, which no speech can be. Speech (and writing) have distanced themselves from the iconic—it is by association, not depiction, that we find speech-poetry evocative; it can elicit moods and images, but it cannot portray them (except through "accidental" ideophones and onomatopoeia). Sign retains a direct power of portrayal that has no analogue in, cannot be translated into, the language of speech; on the other hand, it can ascend to any height of metaphor or trope.

Sign still preserves, and emphasizes, both of its faces—the iconic and the abstract, equally, in complementarity—and thus, while it is able to ascend to the most abstract propositions, to the most generalized reflection of reality, it can also simultaneously evoke a concreteness, a vividness, a realness, an aliveness, that spoken languages, if they ever had, have long since abandoned.[78]

A language's "character," for Humboldt, is essentially cultural—it expresses (and perhaps partly determines) the way a whole people think and feel and aspire. In the case of Sign, the distinctiveness of the language, its "character," is biological as well, for it is rooted in gesture, in iconicity, in a radical visuality, which sets it apart from any spoken tongue. Language arises— biologically—from below, from the irrepressible need of the human individual to think and communicate. But it is also generated, and transmitted—culturally—from above, a living and urgent embodiment of the history, the world-views, the images and passions of a people. Sign for the deaf is a unique adaptation to another sensory mode; but it is also, and equally, an embodiment of their personal and cultural identity. For in the language of a people, Herder observes, "resides its whole thought domain, its tradition, history, religion, and basis of life, all its heart and soul." This is especially true of Sign, for it is not only biologically but culturally—and unsilenceably—the voice of the deaf.

The Revolution of the Deaf

WEDNESDAY *morning, March 9, 1988:* "Strike at Gallaudet," "Deaf Strike for the Deaf," "Students Demand Deaf President"—the media are full of these happenings today; they started three days ago, have been steadily building, and are now on the front page of *The New York Times.* It looks like an amazing story. I have been to Gallaudet University a couple of times in the past year, and have been steadily getting to know the place. Gallaudet is the only liberal arts college for the deaf in the world and is, moreover, the core of the world's deaf community—but, in all its 124 years, it has never had a deaf president.

I flatten out the paper and read the whole story: the students have been actively campaigning for a deaf president ever since the resignation last year of Jerry Lee, a hearing person who had been president since 1984. Unrest, uncertainty, and hope have been brewing. By mid-February, the presidential search committee narrowed the search to six candidates—three hearing, three deaf. On March 1, three thousand people attended a rally at Gallaudet to make it clear to the board of trustees that the Gallaudet community was strongly insisting on the selection of a deaf president. On March 5, the night before the election, a candlelight vigil was held outside the board's quarters. On Sunday, March 6, choosing between three finalists, one hearing, two deaf, the board chose Elisabeth Ann Zinser, Vice-Chancellor for Academic Affairs at the University of North Carolina at Greensboro—the hearing candidate.

The tone, as well as the content, of the board's announcement caused outrage: it was here that the chairman of the board, Jane Bassett Spilman, made her comment that "the deaf are not yet ready to function in the hearing world." The next day, a thousand students marched to the hotel where the board was cloistered, then the six blocks to the White House, and on to the Capitol. The following day, March 8, the students closed the university and barricaded the campus.

Wednesday afternoon: The faculty and staff have come out in support of the students and their four demands: (1) that a new, *deaf* president be named immediately; (2) that the chairman of the board, Jane Bassett Spilman, resign immediately; (3) that the board have a 51 percent majority of deaf members (at present it has seventeen hearing members and only four deaf); and (4) that there be no reprisals. At this point, I phone my friend Bob Johnson. Bob is head of the linguistics department at Gallaudet, where he has taught and done research for seven years. He has a deep knowledge of the deaf and their culture, is an excellent signer, and is married to a deaf woman. He is as close to the deaf community as a hearing person can be.[1] I want to know how he feels about the events at Gallaudet. "It's the most remarkable thing I've ever seen," he says. "If you'd asked me a month ago, I'd have bet a million dollars this couldn't happen in my lifetime. You've got to come down and see this for yourself."

When I had visited Gallaudet in 1986 and 1987, I found it an astonishing and moving experience. I had never before seen an entire community of the deaf, nor had I quite realized (even though I knew this theoretically) that Sign might indeed be a complete language—a language equally suitable for making love or speeches, for flirtation or mathematics. I had to see philosophy and chemistry classes in Sign; I had to see the absolutely silent mathematics department at work; to see deaf bards, Sign poetry, on the campus, and the range and depth of the Gallaudet theater; I had to see the wonderful social scene in the student bar, with hands flying in all directions as a hundred separate conversations proceeded[2]—I had to see all this for myself before I could be moved from my previous "medical" view of deafness (as a condition, a deficit, that had to be "treated") to a "cultural" view of the deaf as forming a community with a complete language and culture of its own. I had felt there was something very joyful, even Arcadian about Gallaudet—and I was not surprised to hear that some of the students were occasionally reluctant to leave its warmth and seclusion and protectiveness, the cosiness of a small but complete and self-sufficient world, for the unkind and uncomprehending big world outside.[3]

But there were also tensions and resentments under the surface, which seemed to be simmering, with no possibility of resolution. There was an unspoken tension between faculty and administration—a faculty in which many of the teachers sign and some are deaf. The faculty could, to some extent, communicate with the students, enter their worlds, their minds; but the administration (so I was told) formed a remote governing body, running the school like a corporation, with a certain "benevolent" caretaker attitude to the "handicapped" deaf, but little real

feeling for them as a community, as a culture. It was feared by
the students and teachers I talked to that the administration, if
it could, would reduce still further the percentage of deaf teachers at Gallaudet and further restrict the teachers' use of Sign
there.[4]

The students I met seemed animated, a lively group when
together, but often fearful and diffident of the outside world. I
had the feeling of some cruel undermining of self-image, even
in those who professed "Deaf Pride." I had the feeling that some
of them thought of themselves as children—an echo of the
parental attitude of the board (and perhaps of some of the faculty). I had the feeling of a certain passivity among them,
a sense that though life might be improved in small ways here
and there, it was their lot to be overlooked, to be second-class
citizens.[5]

Thursday morning, March 10: A taxi deposits me on Eighth
Street opposite the college. The gates have been blocked off for
forty-eight hours; my first sight is of a huge, excited, but cheer-
ful and friendly crowd of hundreds barring the entrance to the
campus, carrying banners and placards, and signing to one
another with great animation. One or two police cars sit parked
outside, watching, their engines purring, but they seem a
benign presence. There is a good deal of honking from the traf-
fic passing by—I am puzzled by this, but then spot a sign reading HONK FOR A DEAF PRESIDENT. The crowd itself is both
strangely silent and noisy: the signing, the Sign speeches, are
utterly silent; but they are punctuated by curious applause—an
excited shaking of the hands above the head, accompanied by
high-pitched vocalizations and screams.[6] As I watch, one of the
students leaps up on a pillar and starts signing with much
expression and beauty. I can understand nothing of what he

says, but I feel the signing is pure and impassioned—his whole body, all his feelings, seem to flow into the signing. I hear a murmured name—Tim Rarus—and realize that this is one of the student leaders, one of the Four. His audience visibly hangs on every sign, rapt, bursting at intervals into tumultuous applause.

As I watch Rarus and his audience, and then let my gaze wander past the barricades to the great campus filled with passionate Sign, with passionate soundless conversation, I get an overwhelming feeling not only of another mode of communication but of another mode of sensibility, another mode of being. One has only to see the students—even casually, from the outside (and I felt quite as much an outsider as those who walked or drove casually by)—to feel that in their language, their mode of being, they *deserve* one of their own, that no one not deaf, not signing, could possibly understand them. One feels, intuitively, that interpretation can never be sufficient—that the students would be cut off from any president who was not one of them.

Innumerable banners and signs catch the brilliant March sun: DEAF PREZ NOW is clearly the basic one. There is a certain amount of anger—it could hardly be otherwise—but the anger, on the whole, is clothed in wit: thus a common sign is DR. ZINSER IS NOT READY TO FUNCTION IN THE DEAF WORLD, a retort to Spilman's malapropos statement about the deaf. Dr. Zinser's own comment on *Nightline* the night before ("A deaf individual, one day, will . . . be president of Gallaudet") had provoked many signs saying: WHY NOT MARCH 10, 1988, DR. ZINSER? The papers have spoken of "battle" or "confrontation," which gives a sense of a negotiation, an inching to and fro. But the students say: "Negotiation? We have forgotten the word. 'Negotiation' no longer appears in our dictionaries." Dr. Zinser keeps asking for a "meaningful dialogue," but this in itself seems a meaningless

request, for there is no longer, there never has been, any intermediate ground on which "dialogue" could take place. The students are concerned with their identity, their survival, an
all-or-none: they have four demands, and there is no place for
"sometime" or "maybe."

Indeed Dr. Zinser is anything but popular. It is felt by many
not only that she is peculiarly insensitive to the mood of the students—the glaring fact that they do not want her, that the university has been literally barricaded against her—but that she
actively stands for and prosecutes an official "hard line." At first
there was a certain sympathy for her: she had been duly chosen
and she had no idea what she had been thrown into. But with
the passing of each day this view grew less and less tenable, and
the whole business began to resemble a contest of wills. Dr.
Zinser's tough, "no-nonsense" stance reached a peak yesterday,
when she loudly asserted that she was going to "take charge" of
the unruly campus. "If it gets any further out of control," she
said, "I'm going to have to take action to bring it under control."
This incensed the students, who promptly burned her in effigy.

Some of the placards are nakedly furious: one says ZINSER—
PUPPET OF SPILMAN, another WE DON'T NEED A WET NURSE,
MOMMY SPILMAN. I begin to realize that this is the deaf's coming
of age, saying at last, in a very loud voice: "We're no longer your
children. We no longer want your 'care.'"[7]

I edge past the barricades, the speeches, the signs, and stroll
onto the large and beautifully green campus, with its great Victorian buildings setting off a most un-Victorian scene. The
campus is buzzing, visibly, with conversation—everywhere
there are pairs or small groups signing. There is conversing
everywhere, and I can understand none of it; *I* feel like the deaf,
the voiceless one today—the handicapped one, the minority, in

this great signing community. I see lots of faculty as well as students on the campus: one professor is making and selling lapel buttons ("Frau Zinser, Go Home!"), which are bought and pinned on as quickly as he makes them. "Isn't this great?" he says, catching sight of me. "I haven't had such a good time since Selma. It feels a little like Selma—and the sixties."

A great many dogs are on the campus—there must be fifty or sixty on the great greensward out front. Regulations on owning and keeping dogs here are loose; some are "hearing ear" dogs, but some are just . . . dogs. I see one girl signing to her dog; the dog, obediently, turns over, begs, gives a paw. This dog itself bears a white cloth sign on each side: I UNDERSTAND SIGN BETTER THAN SPILMAN. (The chairman of Gallaudet's board of trustees has occupied her position for seven years while learning hardly any Sign.)

Where there was a hint of something angry, tense, at the barricades, there is an atmosphere of calm and peacefulness inside; more, a sense of joy, and something like festivity. There are dogs everywhere, and babies and children too, friends and families everywhere, conversing volubly in Sign. There are little colored tents on the grass, and hot dog stands selling frankfurters and soda—dogs and hot dogs: it is rather like Woodstock, much more like Woodstock than a grim revolution.

Earlier in the week, the initial reactions to Elisabeth Ann Zinser's appointment were furious—and uncoordinated; there were a thousand individuals on the campus, milling around, tearing up toilet paper, destructive in mood. But all at once, as Bob Johnson said, "the whole consciousness changed." Within hours there seemed to emerge a new, calm, clear consciousness and resolution; a political body, two thousand strong, with a single, focused will of its own. It was the astonishing swiftness with which this organization emerged, the sudden precipitation, from chaos, of a unanimous, communal mind, that astonished everyone who saw it. And yet, of course, this was partly an illusion, for there were all sorts of preparations—and people—behind it.

Central to this sudden "transformation"—and central, thereafter, in organizing and articulating the entire "uprising" (which was far too dignified, too beautifully modulated, to be called an "uproar")—were the four remarkable young student leaders: Greg Hlibok, the leader of the student body, and his cohorts Tim Rarus, Bridgetta Bourne, and Jerry Covell. Greg Hlibok is a young engineering student, described (by Bob Johnson) as "very engaging, laconic, direct, but in his words a great deal of thought and judgment." Hlibok's father, who is also deaf, runs an engineering firm; his deaf mother, Peggy O'Gorman Hlibok, is active in lobbying for the educational use of ASL; and he has two deaf brothers, one a writer and actor, one a financial consultant, and a deaf sister, also a student at Gallaudet. Tim Rarus, also born deaf, and from a deaf family, is a perfect foil for Greg; he has an eager spontaneity, a passion, an intensity that nicely complement Greg's quietness. The four had already been elected before the uprising—indeed while Jerry Lee was still president—but have taken on a very special, unprecedented role since President Lee's resignation.

Hlibok and his fellow student leaders have not incited or inflamed students—on the contrary, they are calming, restraining, and moderating in their influence, but have been highly sensitive to the "feel" of the campus and, beyond this, of the deaf community at large, and have felt with them that a crucial time has arrived. They have organized the students to press for a deaf president, but they have not done this alone: behind them there has been the active support of alumni, and of deaf organizations and leaders all around the country. Thus, much calculation, much preparation, preceded the "transformation," the emergence of a communal mind. It is not an order appearing from total chaos (even though it might seem so). Rather, it is the sudden manifestation of a latent order, like the sudden crystallization of a super-saturated solution—a crystallization precipitated by the naming of Zinser as president on Sunday night. This is a qualitative transformation, from passivity to activity, and in the moral no less than in the political sense, it is a revolution. Suddenly the deaf are no longer passive, scattered, and powerless; suddenly they have discovered the calm strength of union.

In the afternoon I recruit an interpreter and with her help interview a couple of deaf students. One of them tells me:

> I'm from a hearing family . . . my whole life I've felt pressures, hearing pressures on me—"You can't *do* it in the hearing world, you can't *make* it in the hearing world"—and right now all that pressure is lifted from me. I feel free, all of a sudden, full of energy now. You keep hearing "you can't, you can't," but I *can* now. The words "deaf and dumb" will be destroyed forever; instead there'll be "deaf and able."

These were very much the terms Bob Johnson had used, when we first talked, when he spoke of the deaf as laboring under "an illusion of powerlessness," and of how, all of a sudden, this illusion had been shattered.

Many revolutions, transformations, awakenings are in response to immediate (and intolerable) circumstances. What is so remarkable about the Gallaudet strike of 1988 is its historical consciousness, the sense of deep historical perspective that informs it. That was evident on campus; as soon as I arrived I spotted a picket saying: LAURENT CLERC WANTS DEAF PREZ. HE IS NOT HERE BUT HIS SPIRIT IS HERE. SUPPORT US. I overheard one journalist say, "Who the hell's Laurent Clerc?" but his name, his persona, unknown to the hearing world, are known to virtually everyone in the deaf world. He is a founding father, a heroic figure, in deaf history and culture. The *first* emancipation of the deaf—their achievement of education and literacy, of self-respect and the respect of their fellows—was largely inspired by the achievement and person of Laurent Clerc. It was immensely moving, then, to see this placard, and one could not help feeling that Laurent Clerc *was* here, on the campus, *was*, albeit posthumously, the authentic spirit and voice of the revolt—for he, above all, had laid the foundations of their education and culture.

When Clerc founded the American Asylum at Hartford with Thomas Gallaudet in 1817, he not only introduced Sign as the medium of all deaf schooling in the United States but also introduced a remarkable school system—one that has no exact parallel in the speaking world. Other residential schools for the deaf soon opened throughout the country, all using the Sign that had evolved at Hartford. Virtually all the teachers in these schools were educated at Hartford, and most had met the charismatic Clerc. They contributed their own indigenous signs and later spread an increasingly polished and generalized ASL in many parts of the country, and the standards and aspirations of the deaf continually rose.

The unique pattern of transmission of deaf culture relates equally to the deaf's language (Sign) and to their schools. These schools acted as foci for the deaf community, passing down deaf history and culture from one generation to the next. Their influence went well beyond the classroom: commonly, deaf communities would spring up around the schools, and graduates would often remain close to the school, or even take jobs working in the school. And crucially, most of these schools for the deaf were residential schools, as Carol Padden and Tom Humphries point out:

> The most significant aspect of residential life is the dormitory. In the dormitories, away from the structured control of the classroom, deaf children are introduced to the social life of deaf people. In the informal dormitory environment, children not only learn sign language but the content of the culture. In this way, the schools become hubs of the communities that surround them, preserving for the next generation the culture of earlier generations. . . . This unique pattern of transmission lies at the heart of the culture.[8]

Thus, with great rapidity, in the years after 1817, there spread throughout the States not just a language and a literacy, but a body of shared knowledge, shared beliefs, cherished narratives and images, which soon constituted a rich and distinctive culture. Now, for the first time, there was an "identity" for the deaf, not merely a personal one, but a social, cultural one. They were no longer just individuals, with an individual's plights or triumphs; they were *a people*, with their own culture, like the Jews or the Welsh.[9]

By the 1850s it had become clear that higher education was also needed—the deaf, previously illiterate, now needed a college. In 1857, Thomas Gallaudet's son, Edward, only twenty years old, but uniquely equipped through his background (his mother was deaf, and he learned Sign as a primary language), his sensibilities, and his gifts, was appointed principal of the Columbia Institution for the Instruction of the Deaf and the Dumb and the Blind,[10] conceiving and hoping from the start it could be transformed into a college with federal support. In 1864 this was achieved, and what was later to become Gallaudet College received its charter from Congress.

Edward Gallaudet's own full and extraordinary life lasted well into the present century and spanned great (though not always admirable) changes in attitudes to deaf people and their education. In particular, gathering force from the 1860s and promoted to a large extent in the United States by Alexander Graham Bell was an attitude that opposed the use of signing, and sought to forbid its use in schools and institutions. Gallaudet himself fought against this, but was overborne by the climate of the times, and by a certain ferocity and intransigence of mind that he himself was too reasonable to understand.[11]

By the time of Gallaudet's death, his college was world famous and had shown once and for all that the deaf, given the opportunity and the means, could match the hearing in every sphere of academic activity—and for that matter, in athletic activity, too (the spectacular gym at Gallaudet, designed by Frederick Law Olmsted and opened in 1880, was one of the finest in the country; and the football huddle was actually invented at Gallaudet, for players to pass secret tactics among themselves). But Gallaudet himself was one of the last defenders of Sign in an educational world that had turned its back on signing, and with his death the college lost—and because the college had become the symbol and aspiration of the deaf all over the world, the deaf world also lost—its greatest and last proponent of Sign in education.

With this, Sign, which had been the dominant language at the college before, went underground and became confined to a colloquial use.[12] The students continued to use it among themselves, but it was no longer considered a legitimate language for formal discourse or teaching. Thus the century between Thomas Gallaudet's founding of the American Asylum and Edward Gallaudet's death in 1917 saw the rise and fall, the legitimation and delegitimation, of Sign in America.[13]

The suppression of Sign in the 1880s had a deleterious effect on the deaf for seventy-five years, not only on their education and academic achievements but on their image of themselves and on their entire community and culture. Such community and culture as did exist remained in isolated pockets—there was no longer the sense there had once been, at least the sense that was intimated in the "golden age" of the 1840s, of a nationwide (even worldwide) community and culture.

But the last thirty years have again seen a reversal—and indeed a relegitimation and resurrection of Sign as never before; and with this, and much else, a discovery or rediscovery of the cultural aspects of deafness—a strong sense of community and communication and culture, of a self-definition as a unique mode of being.

De l'Epée had immense admiration, but also reservations, about sign language: on the one hand, he saw it as a complete form of communication ("Every deaf-mute sent to us already has a language . . . with it, he expresses his needs, desires, pains, and so on, and makes no mistake when others express themselves likewise"), on the other, as lacking inner structure, a grammar (which he tried to inject, from French, with his "methodical signs"). This strange mixture of admiration and denigration continued for the next two hundred years, even among the deaf. But it is likely that, until William Stokoe came to Gallaudet in 1955, no linguist had really confronted the reality of Sign.

One may speak of "the revolution of 1988" and feel, as Bob Johnson did, as, in a sense, everyone did, that this was an astounding event, a transformation, that could hardly have been expected in our lifetimes. At one level, indeed, this is true; but at another level one must see that the movement, the many movements that flowed together to create the explosion of 1988, were many years in the gathering, and that the seeds of the revolution were planted thirty years ago (if not a hundred and fifty years ago). It will be a complex task to reconstruct the history of the past thirty years, specifically the new chapter of deaf history which may be considered to have started in 1960 with Stokoe's "bombshell" paper on *Sign Language Structure*, the first-ever serious and scientific attention paid to "the visual communication system of the American deaf."

I have spoken about this complex prehistory of the revolution, the complex and tangled skein of events and changing attitudes that preceded it, to many people: to the students at Gallaudet; to historians like Harlan Lane, and John Van Cleve (who compiled the enormous three-volume *Gallaudet Encyclopedia of Deaf People and Deafness*); to researchers like William Stokoe, Ursula Bellugi, Michael Karchmer, Bob Johnson, Hilde Schlesinger, and many others; and no two of them see it the same way.[14]

Stokoe's own passions were those of a scientist—but a scientist of language is a special sort of creature who needs to be as interested in human life, in human community and culture, as he is in the biological determinants of language. This doubleness of interest and approach led Stokoe, in his 1965 *Dictionary*, to include an appendix (by his deaf collaborator, Carl Croneberg) on "The Linguistic Community," the first description of the social and cultural characteristics of deaf people who used American Sign Language. Writing of the *Dictionary* fifteen years later, Padden saw it as a "landmark":

> It was unique to describe "Deaf people" as constituting a cultural group . . . it represented a break from the long tradition of "pathologizing" Deaf people. . . . In a sense the book brought official and public recognition of a deeper aspect of Deaf people's lives: their culture.

But though, in retrospect, Stokoe's works were seen as "bombshells" and "landmarks," and though, in retrospect, they can be seen as having had a major part in leading to the subsequent transformation of consciousness, they were all but ignored at the time. Stokoe himself, looking back, commented wryly:[15]

> Publication in 1960 [of *Sign Language Structure*] brought a curious local reaction. With the exception of Dean Detmold and one or two colleagues, the entire Gallaudet College faculty rudely attacked me, linguistics, and the study of signing as a language. . . . If the reception of the first linguistic study of a Sign Language of the deaf community was chilly at home, it was cryogenic in a large part of special education—at that time a closed corporation as hostile to Sign Language, as [it was] ignorant of linguistics.

There was certainly very little impact among his fellow linguists: the great general works on language of the 1960s make
no reference to it—or indeed to Sign at all. Nor did Chomsky,
the most revolutionary linguist of our time, when, in 1966, he
promised (in the preface to *Cartesian Linguistics*) a future book
on "language surrogates . . . for example, the gesture language
of the deaf"—a description that placed Sign below the category
of real language.[16] And when Klima and Bellugi themselves
turned to the study of Sign, in 1970, they had the feeling of vir-
gin soil, of a totally new subject (this was partly a reflection of
their own originality, the originality that makes every subject
seem totally new).

More remarkable, in a sense, was the indifferent or hostile
reaction of the deaf themselves, whom one might have thought
would have been the first to see and welcome Stokoe's insights.
There are intriguing descriptions of this—and of later "conver-
sions"—provided by former colleagues of Stokoe, and others, all
of whom were themselves native signers, either deaf or born of
deaf parents. Would not a signer be the first to see the structural complexity of his own language? But it was precisely
signers who were most uncomprehending, or most resistant to
Stokoe's notions. Thus Gilbert Eastman (later to become an
eminent Sign playwright, and a most ardent supporter of
Stokoe's) tells us, "My colleagues and I laughed at Dr. Stokoe
and his crazy project. It was impossible to analyze our Sign
Language."

The reasons for this are complex and deep and may not have
any parallel in the hearing-speaking world. For we (99.9 percent of us) take speech and spoken language for granted; we
have no special interest in speech, we never give it a second
thought, nor do we care whether it is analyzed or not. But it is

profoundly different for the deaf and Sign. They have a special, intense feeling for their own language: they tend to extol it in tender, reverent terms (and have done so since Desloges, in 1779). The deaf feel Sign as a most intimate, indissociable part of their being, as something they depend on, and also, frighteningly, as something that may be taken from them at any time (as it was, in a way, by the Milan conference in 1880). They are, as Padden and Humphries say, suspicious of "the science of others," which they feel may overpower their own knowledge of Sign, a knowledge that is "impressionistic, global, and not internally analytic." Yet, paradoxically, with all this reverent feeling, they have often shared the hearing's incomprehension or depreciation of Sign. (One of the things that most impressed Bellugi, when she launched on her own studies, was that the deaf themselves, while native signers, often had no idea of the grammar or inner structure of Sign and tended to see it as pantomime.)

And yet, perhaps, this is not so surprising. There is an old proverb that fish are the last to recognize water. And for signers, Sign is their medium and water, so familiar and natural to them, as to need no explanation. The users of a language, above all, will tend to a naive realism, to see their language as a reflection of reality, not as a construct. "The aspects of things that are most important to us are hidden because of their simplicity and familiarity," Wittgenstein says. Thus it may take an outside view to show the native users of a language that their own utterances, which appear so simple and transparent to themselves, are, in fact, enormously complex and contain and conceal the vast apparatus of a true language. This is precisely what happened with Stokoe and the deaf—and it is put clearly by Louie Fant:

Like most children of deaf parents, I grew up with no conscious awareness that ASL was a language. It was not until
my mid-thirties that I was relieved of this misconception. My
enlightenment came from people who were not native users of
ASL—who had come into the field of deafness with no pre-
conceived notions, and bound to no points of view regarding
deaf people and their language. They looked at the signed language of the deaf with fresh eyes.

Fant goes on to describe how despite working at Gallaudet
and getting to know Stokoe well (and even himself writing a
sign language primer using some of Stokoe's analysis), he still
resisted the idea that it was a real language. When he left Gallaudet to become a founding member of the National Theater of
the Deaf, in 1967, this attitude persisted among him and others—all productions were in signed English, because ASL was
considered "bastardized English not fit for the stage." Once or
twice Fant, and others, almost inadvertently used ASL in
declaiming on stage, with electric effect, and this had a strange
effect on them. "Somewhere in the recesses of my mind," Fant
writes of this time, "was a growing awareness that Bill was
right, and that what we called 'real Sign Language' was in fact
ASL."

But it was only in 1970, when Fant met Klima and Bellugi,
who asked him innumerable questions about "his" language,
that the change occurred:

As the conversation proceeded, my attitude underwent a complete conversion. In her warm, winning way, she [Bellugi]
made me realize how little I really knew about Sign Language, even though I had known it from childhood. Her praise

for Bill Stokoe and his work made me wonder if I was missing something.

And then, finally, a few weeks later:

I became a convert. I ceased to resist the idea that ASL was a language, and submerged myself in studying it so that I could teach it as a language.

And yet—despite talk of "conversion"—deaf people have always known, intuitively, that Sign was a language. But perhaps it required a scientific confirmation before this knowledge could become conscious and explicit, and form the basis of a bold and new consciousness of their own language.

Artists (Pound reminds us) are the antennae of the race. And it was artists who first felt in themselves, and announced, the dawn of this new consciousness. Thus the first movement to stem from Stokoe's work was not educational, not political, not social, but artistic. The National Theater of the Deaf (NTD) was founded in 1967, just two years after the publication of the *Dictionary*. But it was only in 1973, six years later, that the NTD commissioned, and performed, a play in true Sign; up to that point, their productions had merely been transliterations, in signed English, of English plays. (Although during the 1950s and 1960s, George Detmold, dean of Gallaudet College, produced a number of plays in which he urged the actors to move away from signed English and perform in ASL.[17]) Once the resistance had been broken, and the new consciousness established, there was no stopping deaf artists of all sorts. There arose Sign poetry, Sign wit, Sign song, Sign dance—unique Sign arts that could not be translated into speech. A bardic tra-

dition arose, or re-arose, among the deaf, with Sign bards, Sign
orators, Sign storytellers, Sign narrators, who served to transmit and disseminate the history and culture of the deaf, and, in
so doing, raise the new cultural consciousness yet higher. The
NTD traveled, and still travels, all over the world, not only
introducing deaf art and culture to the hearing but reaffirming
the deaf's feeling of having a world community and culture.

Though art is art, and culture is culture, they may have an
implicitly (if not an explicitly) political and educational function. Fant himself became a protagonist and teacher; his 1972
book *Ameslan: An Introduction to American Sign Language* was the
first Sign primer on explicitly Stokoean lines; it was a force in
assisting the return of signed language to education. In the
early 1970s the exclusive oralism of ninety-six years began to
be reversed, and "total communication" (the use of both signed
and spoken language) was introduced (or reintroduced, as it had
been common enough, in many countries, a hundred and fifty
years before).[18] This was not accomplished without great resistance. Schlesinger tells us that when she advocated the rein-
troduction of signed languages in education, she received
warnings and threatening letters, and that when her book
Sound and Sign appeared in 1972, it caused controversy and
tended to be "wrapped in a plain brown wrapper as if unaccept-
able." And even now the conflict still rages unresolved, and
though signed language is now used in schools, *it is virtually
always signed English and not Sign that is used.* Stokoe had said
from the first that the deaf should be bilingual (and bicultural),
should acquire the language of the dominant culture, but also
and equally their own language, Sign.[19] But since Sign is still
not used in schools, or in any institutions (except religious
ones), it is still largely restricted, as seventy years ago, to a col-

loquial and demotic use. This is even the case at Gallaudet itself—indeed, it has been the university's official policy since 1982 that all signing and interpretation in class be conducted in signed English—and this constituted an important contributing reason for the revolt.

The personal and the political are always combined, and here both are combined with the linguistic too. Barbara Kannapell brings this out when she traces the influence of Stokoe, of the new consciousness, on herself and how she became aware of herself as a deaf person with a special linguistic identity—"my language is me"—and moved from this to seeing Sign as central to the communal identity of the deaf ("To reject ASL is to reject the deaf person . . . [for] ASL is a personal creation of deaf persons as a group . . . it is the only thing we have that belongs to deaf people completely"). Moved by these personal and social considerations, Kannapell founded Deaf Pride, an organization dedicated to deaf consciousness-raising, in 1972.

Deaf depreciation, deaf deference, deaf passivity, and even deaf shame were all too common before the early 1970s; one sees this, very clearly, in the 1970 novel by Joanne Greenberg, *In This Sign*—and it took Stokoe's dictionary, and the legitimation of Sign by linguists, to allow the beginnings of a movement in the opposite direction, a movement toward deaf identity and deaf pride.

This was essential, but, of course, not the only factor in the deaf movement since 1960: there were many other factors of equal force, and all flowed together to produce the revolution of 1988. There was the mood of the sixties, with its special feeling for the poor, the disabled, the minorities—the civil rights movement, the political activism, the varied "pride" and "liberation" movements; all this was afoot at the same time that Sign was slowly, and against much resistance, being legitimated scientifically, and while the deaf were slowly collecting a sense of self-esteem and hope, and fighting against the negative images and feelings that had dogged them for a century. There was an increasing tolerance, generally, for cultural diversity, an increasing sense that peoples could be profoundly different, yet all be valuable and equal to one another; an increasing sense, specifically, that the deaf *were* a "people," and not merely a number of isolated, abnormal, disabled individuals; a movement from the medical or pathological view to an anthropological, sociological, or ethnic view.[20]

Going along with this depathologizing was an increase in portrayals of deaf people in every medium, from documentaries to plays and novels—a portrayal increasingly sympathetic and imaginative. Changing social attitudes and changing self-image were both reflected in, and affected by, these: the image ceased to be that of the diffident and pathetic Mr. Singer in *The Heart is a Lonely Hunter* and became the audacious heroine of *Children of a Lesser God*; Sign was introduced on television, in such programs as "Sesame Street," and started to become a popular elective at some schools. The entire country became more aware of the previously invisible and inaudible deaf; and they too became more aware of themselves, of their increasing visibility and power in society. Deaf people, and those who studied them, started to look back into the past—to discover (or create) a deaf history, a deaf mythology, a deaf heritage.[21]

Thus, within twenty years of Stokoe's paper, new awareness, new motives, new forces of all sorts were combining—a new movement was afoot, a confrontation was in the making. The 1970s saw the rise not only of Deaf Pride but of Deaf Power. Leaders arose among the previously passive deaf. A new vocabulary arose, with such words as "self-determination" and "paternalism" in it. The deaf, who had previously accepted characterizations of themselves as "disabled" and "dependent"—for this is how they had been regarded by the hearing—now started to think of themselves as powerful, as an autonomous community.[22] Sooner or later, it was clear, there would have to be a revolt, a striking political assertion of self-determination and independence, and a once-and-for-all repudiation of paternalism.

The accusation that the Gallaudet authorities were "deaf in the mind" implies no malevolence, but rather a misdirected paternalism, which, deaf people feel, is anything but benign—based as it is on pity and condescension, and on an implicit view of them as "incompetent," if not diseased. Special objection has been made to some of the doctors involved in Gallaudet's affairs, who, it is felt, tend to see the deaf merely as having diseased ears and not as whole people adapted to another sensory mode. In general, it is felt this offensive benevolence hinges on a value judgment by the hearing, their saying: "We know what is best for you. Let *us* handle things," whether this is in response to the choice of language (allowing, or not allowing, Sign), or in judging capacities for education or jobs. It is still sometimes felt, or again felt—after the more spacious opportunities offered in the mid-nineteenth century—that deaf people should be printers, or work in the post office, do "humble" jobs and not aspire to higher education. The deaf, in other words, felt they were being dictated to, that they were being treated as children. Bob Johnson told me a typical story:

It's been my impression, after having been here for several years, that the Gallaudet faculty and staff treat students as pets. One student, for example, went to the Outreach office; they had announced there would be an opportunity to practice interviewing for jobs. The idea was to sign up for a genuine interview and learn how to do it. So he went and put his name on a list. The next day a woman from the Outreach office called and told him she had set up the interview, had found an interpreter, had set up the time, had arranged for a car to take him . . . and she couldn't understand why he got mad at her. He told her, "The reason I was doing this was so that I could learn how to call the person, and learn how to get the car, and learn how to get the interpreter, and you're doing it for me. That's not what I want here." That's the meat of the issue.

Far from being childlike or incompetent, as they were "supposed" to be (and so often they supposed themselves to be), the students at Gallaudet showed high competence in managing the March revolt. This impressed me especially when I wandered into the communications room, the nerve-center of Gallaudet during the strike, with its central office filled with TTY-equipped telephones.[23] Here the deaf students contacted the press and television—invited them in, gave interviews, compiled news, issued press releases, round the clock—masterfully; here they raised funds for a "Deaf Prez Now" campaign; here they solicited, successfully, support from Congress, presidential candidates, union leaders. They gained the world's ear, at this extraordinary time, when they needed it.

Even the administration listened—so that after four days of seeing the students as foolish and rebellious children who needed to be brought into line, Dr. Zinser was forced to pause, to listen, to reexamine her own long-held assumptions, to see things in a new light—and, finally, to resign. She did so in terms that were moving and seemed genuine, saying that neither she nor the board had anticipated the fervor and commitment of the protesters, or that their protest was the leading edge of a burgeoning national movement for deaf rights. "I have responded to this extraordinary social movement of deaf people," she said as she tendered her resignation on the night of March 10 and spoke of coming to see this as "a very special moment in time," one that was "unique, a civil rights moment in history for deaf people."

Friday, March 11: The mood on campus is completely transformed. A battle has been won. There is elation. More battles have to be fought. Placards with the students' four demands have been replaced with placards saying, "3 1/2," because the resignation of Dr. Zinser only goes halfway toward meeting the first demand, that there be a deaf president immediately. But there is also a gentleness that is new, the tension and anger of Thursday have gone, along with the possibility of a drawn-out, humiliating defeat. A largeness of spirit is everywhere apparent—released now, I partly feel, by the grace and the words with which Zinser resigned, words in which she aligned herself with, and wished the best for, what she called an "extraordinary social movement."

Support is coming in from every quarter: three hundred deaf students from the National Technical Institute for the Deaf arrive, elated and exhausted, after a fifteen-hour bus ride from Rochester, New York. Deaf schools throughout the country are closed in total support. Deaf people flood in from every state—I see signs from Iowa and Alabama, from Canada, from South America, as well as from Europe, even from New Zealand. Events at Gallaudet have dominated the national press for forty-eight hours. Virtually every car going past Gallaudet honks now, and the streets are filled with supporters as the time for the march on the Capitol comes near. And yet, for all the honking, the speeches, the banners, the pickets, an extraordinary atmosphere of quietness and dignity prevails.

Noon: There are now about 2,500 people, a thousand students from Gallaudet and the rest supporters, as we start on a slow march to the Capitol. As we walk a wonderful sense of quietness grows, which puzzles me. It is not wholly physical (indeed, there is rather a lot of noise in a way—the ear-splitting yells of the deaf, as a start), and I decide it is, rather, the quietness of a moral drama. The sense of history in the air gives it this strange quietness.

Slowly, for there are children, babes-in-arms, and some physically disabled among us (some deaf-blind, some ataxic, and some on crutches)—slowly, and with a mixed sense of resolve and festivity, we walk to the Capitol, and there, in the clear March sun that has shone the entire week, we unfurl banners and raise pickets. One great banner says WE STILL HAVE A DREAM, and another, with the individual letters carried by fourteen people, simply says: HELP US CONGRESS.

We are packed together, but there is no sense of a crowd, rather of an extraordinary camaraderie. Just before the speeches start, I find myself hugged—I think it must be someone I know, but it is a student bearing a sign ALABAMA, who hugs me, punches my shoulder, smiles, as a comrade. We are strangers, but yet, at this special moment, we are comrades.

There are many speeches—from Greg Hlibok, from some of the faculty, from congressmen and senators. I listen for a while:

It is an irony [says one, a professor at Gallaudet] that Gallaudet has never had a deaf chief executive officer. Virtually every black college has a black president, testimony that black people are leading themselves. Virtually every women's college has a woman as president, as testimony that women are capable of leading themselves. It's long past time that Gallaudet had a deaf president as testimony that deaf people are leading themselves.

I let my attention wander, taking in the scene as a whole: thousands of people, each intensely individual, but bound and united with a single sentiment. After the speeches, there is a break of an hour, during which a number of people go in to see congressmen. But most of the group, who have brought packed lunches in on their backs, now sit and eat and talk, or rather sign, in the great plaza before the Capitol—and this, for me, as for all those who have come or chanced to see it, is one of the most wonderful scenes of all. For here are a thousand or more people signing freely, in a public place—not privately, at home, or in the enclosure of Gallaudet—but openly and unself-consciously, and beautifully, before the Capitol.

The press has reported all the speeches, but missed what is surely equally significant. They failed to give the watching world an actual vision of the fullness and vividness, the unmedical life, of the deaf. And once more, as I wander among the huge throng of signers, as they chat over sandwiches and sodas before the Capitol, I find myself remembering the words of a deaf student at the California School for the Deaf, who had signed on television:

> We are a unique people, with our own culture, our own language—American Sign Language, which has just recently been recognized as a language in itself—and that sets us apart from hearing people.

I walk back from the Capitol with Bob Johnson. I myself tend to be apolitical and have difficulty even comprehending the vocabulary of politics. Bob, a pioneer Sign linguist, who has taught and researched at Gallaudet for years, says as we walk back:

> It's really remarkable, because in all my experience I've seen deaf people be passive and accept the kind of treatment that hearing people give them. I've seen them willing, or seem to be willing, to be "clients," when in fact they should be controlling things . . . now all at once there's been a transformation in the consciousness of what it means to be a deaf person in the world, to take responsibility for things. The illusion that deaf people are powerless—all at once, now, that illusion has gone, and that means the whole nature of things can change for them now. I'm very optimistic and extremely enthusiastic about what I'm going to see over the next few years.

"I don't quite understand what you mean by 'clients,'" I say.

> You know Tim Rarus [Bob explains]—the one you saw at the barricades this morning, whose signing you so admired as pure and passionate—well, he summed up in two words what

this transformation is all about. He said, "It's very simple. No deaf president, no university," and then he shrugged his shoulders, looked at the TV cameras, and that was his whole statement. That was the first time deaf people ever realized that a colonial client-industry like this can't exist without the client. It's a billion-dollar industry for hearing people. If deaf people don't participate, the industry is gone.

Saturday has a delightful, holiday air about it—it is a day off (some of the students have been working virtually nonstop from the first demonstration on Sunday evening), and a day for cookouts on the campus. But even here the issues are not forgotten. The very names of the foods have a satirical edge: the choice lies between "Spilman dogs" and "Board burgers." The campus is festive now that students and schoolchildren from a score of other states have come in (a little deaf black girl from Arkansas, seeing all the signers around her, says in Sign, "It's like a family to me today"). There has also been an influx of deaf artists from all over, some coming to document and celebrate this unique event in the history of the deaf.

Greg Hlibok is relaxed, but very vigilant: "We feel that we are in control. We are taking things easy. We don't want to go too far." Two days earlier, Zinser was threatening to "take control." What one sees today is self-control, that quiet consciousness and confidence that comes from an inner strength and certainty.

Sunday evening, March 13: The board met today, for nine hours. There were nine hours of tension, waiting . . . no one knowing what was to come. Then the door opened, and Philip Bravin, one of the four deaf board members and known to all the deaf students, appeared. His appearance—and not

Spilman's—already told the story, before he made his revelations in Sign. He was speaking now, he signed, as chairman of the board, for Spilman had resigned. And his first task now, with the board behind him, was the happy one of announcing that King Jordan had been elected the new president.

King Jordan, deafened at the age of twenty-one, has been at Gallaudet for fifteen years; he is dean of the School of Arts and Sciences, a popular, modest, and unusually sane man, who at first supported Zinser when she was selected.[24] Greatly moved, Jordan, in simultaneous Sign and speech, says:

> I am *thrilled* to accept the invitation of the board of trustees to become the president of Gallaudet University. This is a historic moment for deaf people around the world. This week we can truly say that we together, united, have overcome our reluctance to stand for our rights. The world has watched the deaf community come of age. We will no longer accept limits on what we can achieve. The highest praise goes to the students of Gallaudet for showing us exactly even now how one can seize an idea with such force that it becomes a reality.

With this, the dam bursts, and jubilation bursts out everywhere. As everyone returns to Gallaudet for a final, triumphal meeting, Jordan says, "They know now that the cap on what they can achieve has been lifted. We know that deaf people can do anything hearing people can except hear." And Hlibok, hugging Jordan, adds, "We have climbed to the top of the mountain, and we have climbed together."

Monday, March 14: Gallaudet looks normal on the surface. The barricades have been taken down, the campus is open. The "uprising" has lasted exactly one week—from last Sunday evening, March 6th, when Dr. Zinser was forced on an unwilling university, to the happy resolution last night, that utterly different Sunday evening, when all was changed.

"It took seven days to create the world, it took us seven days to change it"—this was the joke of the students, flashed in Sign from one end of the campus to another. And with this feeling they took their spring break, going back to their families throughout the country, carrying the euphoric news and mood with them.

But objective change, historical change, does not happen in a week, even though its first prerequisite, "the transformation of consciousness," may happen, as it did, in a day. "Many of the students," Bob Johnson told me, "don't realize the extent and the time that are going to be involved in changing, though they do have a sense now of their strength and power. . . . The structure of oppression is so deeply engrained."

And yet there are beginnings. There is a new "image" and a new movement, not merely at Gallaudet but throughout the deaf world. News reports, especially on television, have made the deaf articulate and visible across the entire nation. But the profoundest effect, of course, has been on the deaf themselves. It has welded them into a community, a worldwide community, as never before.[25]

There has already been a deep impact, if only symbolic, upon deaf children. One of King Jordan's first acts, when the college reconvened after spring break, was to visit the grade school at Gallaudet and talk to the children there, something no president had ever done before. Such concern has to affect their perception of what they can become. (Deaf children sometimes think they will "turn into" hearing adults, or else be feeble, put-upon creatures if they do not.) Charlotte, in Albany, watched the events at Gallaudet on television with great excitement, donned a "Deaf Power" T-shirt, and practiced a "Deaf Power" salute. And two months after the revolt at Gallaudet I found myself attending the annual graduation at the Lexington School for the Deaf, which has been a stronghold of oral education since the 1860s. Greg Hlibok, an alumnus, had been invited as the guest speaker (signer); Philip Bravin was also invited; and all the commencement speeches, for the first time in one hundred and twenty years, were given in Sign. None of this would have been conceivable without the Gallaudet revolt.

All sorts of changes, administrative, educational, social, psychological, are already beginning at Gallaudet. But what is clearest at this point is the much-altered bearing of its students, a bearing that conveys a new, wholly unself-conscious sense of pleasure and vindication, of confidence and dignity. This new sense of themselves represents a decisive break from the past, which could not have been imagined just a few months ago.

But has all been changed? Will there be a lasting "transformation of consciousness"? Will deaf people at Gallaudet, and the deaf community at large, indeed find the opportunities they seek? Will we, the hearing, allow them these opportunities? Allow them to be themselves, a unique culture in our midst, yet admit them as co-equals, to every sphere of activity? One hopes the events at Gallaudet will be but the beginning.

Notes

Preface

1. Although the term "Sign" is usually used to denote American Sign Language (ASL), I use it in this book to refer to all indigenous signed languages, past and present (e.g., American Sign Language, French Sign, Chinese Sign, Yiddish Sign, and Old Kentish Sign). But it excludes signed forms of spoken languages (e.g., Signed English), which are mere transliterations and lack the structure of genuine sign languages.

2. Some in the deaf community mark this distinction by a convention whereby audiological deafness is spelled with a small "d," to distinguish it from Deafness with a big "d," as a linguistic and cultural entity.

3. The many (and sometimes lengthy) endnotes should be regarded as mental or imaginative excursions, to be taken, or avoided, as the reader-traveler chooses.

Part I: A Deaf World

1. This colleague, Lucy K., is so expert a speaker and lip-reader that I did not realize at first that she was deaf. It was only when I chanced one

day to turn my head to one side as we were talking, inadvertently cutting off communication instantly, that I realized she was not hearing me but lip-reading me ("lip-reading" is an extremely inadequate word for the complex art of observation, inference, and inspired guesswork which goes on). When the diagnosis of deafness was made, at about twelve months, Lucy's parents had immediately expressed their passionate desire that their daughter should speak and be a part of the hearing world, and her mother devoted hours every day to an intensive one-to-one tuition of speech—a grueling business that lasted twelve years. It was only after this (at the age of fourteen) that Lucy learned Sign; it has always been a second language, and one that does not come "naturally" to her. She continued (with her excellent lip-reading and powerful hearing aids) in "normal" (hearing) classes in high school and college, and now works, with hearing patients, at our hospital. She herself has mixed feelings about her status: "I sometimes feel," she once said, "that I am between two worlds, that I don't quite fit into either."

2. Prior to reading Lane's book, I had seen the few deaf patients under my care in purely medical terms—as "diseased ears" or "otologically impaired." After reading it, I started to see them in a different light, especially when I would catch sight of three or four of them signing, full of an intensity, an animation, I had failed to see before. Only then did I start thinking of them not as deaf but as Deaf, as members of a different linguistic community.

3. There have been at least a half dozen major programs in England since "Voices from Silent Hands" (Horizon, 1980). There have been many programs in the United States (in particular, some excellent ones from Gallaudet University, such as "Hands Full of Words")—the most recent and important of these is Frederick Wiseman's huge, four-part documentary "Deaf and Blind," shown on public television in 1988. There have also been an increasing number of fictional representations of deafness on television. Thus a January 1989 episode of the new "Star Trek," entitled "Louder than a Whisper," featured the deaf actor Howie Seago as a deaf, signing ambassador from another planet.

4. This was indeed the case when Wright's book was published in 1969. Since then there has been an explosion of writings about deaf-

ness by the deaf, of which the most remarkable is *Deaf in America: Voices from a Culture*, by the deaf linguists Carol Padden and Tom Humphries. There have also been novels about the deaf by the deaf, for example, *Islay* by Douglas Bullard, which attempt to catch the distinctive perceptions, the stream of consciousness, the inner speech of those who sign. For other books by deaf writers, see the fascinating bibliography provided by Wright in *Deafness*.

5. Wright uses Wordsworth's phrase, "eye-music," for such experiences, even when there is no accompanying auditory phantasm, and this is used by several deaf writers as a metaphor for their sense of visual patterns and beauty. It is especially used of the recurrent motifs (the "rhymes," the "consonances," etc.) of Sign poetry.

6. There is, of course, a "consensus" of the senses—objects are heard, seen, felt, smelt, all at once, simultaneously; their sound, sight, smell, feel all go together. This correspondence is established by experience and association. This is not, normally, something we are conscious of, although we would be very startled if something didn't sound like it looked—if one of our senses gave a discrepant impression. But we may be *made* conscious, very suddenly and startlingly, of the senses' correspondence, if we are suddenly deprived of a sense, or gain one. Thus David Wright "heard" speech, the moment he was deafened; an anosmic patient of mine "smelt" flowers, whenever he saw them (Sacks,1985); and a patient described by Richard Gregory (in "Recovery from early blindness: a case study," reprinted in Gregory, 1974) could at once read the time on a clock when he was given his sight (he had been blind from birth) by an eye operation: before that he had been used to feeling the hands of a watch with its watch-glass removed, but could make an instant "transmodal" transfer of this knowledge from the tactile to the visual, as soon as he was able to see.

7. This hearing (that is, imagining) of "phantasmal voices," when lips are read, is quite characteristic of the *postlingually* deaf, for whom speech (and "inner speech") has once been an auditory experience. This is not "imagining" in the ordinary sense, but rather an instant and automatic "translation" of the visual experience into an auditory correlate (based on experience and association)—a translation that

probably has a neurological basis (of experientially established visual-auditory connections). This does not occur, of course, in the *prelingually* deaf, who have no auditory experience or imagery to call upon. For them lipreading—as, indeed, ordinary reading—is an entirely visual experience; they see, but do not hear, the voice. It is difficult for us, as speaker-hearers, even to conceive such a visual "voice," as it is for those who have never heard to conceive an auditory voice.

The congenitally deaf, it should be added, may have the richest appreciation of (say) written English, of Shakespeare, even though it does not "speak" to them in an auditory way. It speaks to them, one must suppose, in an entirely visual way—they do not hear, they *see*, the "voice" of the words.

When we read, or imagine someone speaking, we "hear" a voice, upon the inward ear. What of those born deaf? How do they imagine voices? Clayton Valli, a deaf Sign poet, when a poem is coming to him, feels his body making little signs—he is, as it were, speaking to himself, in his own voice. But what if *other* voices are imagined, or dreamed, or hallucinated? The mad often suffer from "hearing voices"—other voices, often accusing voices, nagging and cajoling them; do deaf people, if they go mad, suffer from "seeing voices" too? And, if so, how are these seen? As hands in mid-air making signs; or as whole-body visual apparitions making signs? I have found it oddly difficult to get a clear answer—as it may be difficult, sometimes, to get a dreamer to tell you how he dreams. He is given to understand something, in the course of his dream, but whether by sight or sound, *how*, he is unable to say. There are as yet too few studies on hallucinations, dreaming, and language imagery in the deaf.

The question of how much the postlingually deaf may continue to "hear" has analogies to the ways in which those blinded late in life may continue to "see," and continue, one way and another, in waking and dreams, to live in a visual world. The most extraordinary autobiographical account of this has been provided by John Hull (1990). "During the first couple of years of blindness," he writes, "when I thought about people I knew, they fell into two groups. There are those with faces, and those without faces. . . . The people I knew before I lost my sight have faces but the people I have met since do not have faces . . . as time went by, the proportion of people with no faces increased." With those whom he knew, there would be vivid images of their faces as they spoke to him—though images fixed by his last impressions before he became blind, and therefore increasingly out- dated. With others, of whom there were no actual visual memories, there were, at one point, incontinent visual "projections" (perhaps analogous to Wright's auditory "phantasms" and the phantom limbs of amputees: such "sensory ghosts" are created by the brain when it is suddenly cut off from normal sensory input).

In general, Hull found, as the years went by, he moved deeper and deeper into what he calls "deep blindness," with less and less memory of, imagination of, or need for, visual images, and more and more the sense of being a "whole body seer," living in an autonomous and com- plete world of body sensations, touch, smell, and taste, and, of course, hearing—all these senses now greatly enhanced. He continues to use visual images and metaphors in his speech, but these, increasingly, are only metaphors for him. It is probable that those who have been deaf- ened late in life, similarly, may gradually lose more and more of their auditory memories and images, as they advance into the exclusively visual world of "deep" deafness. When Wright was asked if he would like his hearing back, at this stage, he answered, no, he now found his world complete.

8. This is the stereotypical view, and it is not altogether true. The con- genitally deaf do not experience or complain of "silence" (any more than the blind experience or complain of "darkness"). These are our projections, or metaphors, for their state. Moreover, those with the profoundest deafness may hear noise of various sorts and may be highly sensitive to vibrations of all kinds. This sensitivity to vibration can become a sort of accessory sense: thus Lucy K., although pro- foundly deaf, can immediately judge a chord as a "fifth" by placing a hand on the piano and can interpret voices on highly amplified tele- phones; in both cases what she seems to perceive are vibrations, not sounds. The development of vibration-perception as an accessory sense has some analogies to the development of "facial vision" (which uses the face to receive a sort of sonar information) in the blind.

Hearing people tend to perceive vibrations *or* sound: thus a very low C (below the bottom of the piano scale) might be heard as a low C *or* a toneless fluttering of sixteen vibrations per second. An octave below this, we would hear only fluttering; an octave above this (thirty-two vibrations a second), we would hear a low note with no fluttering. The perception of "tone" within the hearing range is a sort of synthetic judgment or construct of the normal auditory system (see Helmholtz's *The Sensations of Tone,* first published in 1862). If this cannot be achieved, as in the profoundly deaf, there may be an apparent extension of vibratory-sense upward, into realms which, for hearing people, are perceived as tones—even into the middle range of music and speech.

9. Isabelle Rapin thinks of deafness as a treatable, or, better, preventable form of mental retardation (see Rapin, 1979).

There are fascinating differences in style, in approach to the world, between the deaf and the blind (and the normal). Blind children, in particular, tend to become "hyperverbal," to employ elaborate verbal descriptions instead of visual images, trying to deny, or replace, visuality by verbality. This tended, the analyst Dorothy Burlingham thought, to produce a sort of pseudo-visual "false self," a pretense that the child was seeing when it was not (Burlingham, 1972). She felt it crucial to see blind children as having an entirely different profile and "style"—one that required a different sort of education and language—to see them not as deficient, but as different and distinctive in their own right. This was a revolutionary attitude in the 1930s, when her first studies were published. One wishes there were comparable psychoanalytic studies of children born deaf—but this would need a psychoanalyst who, if herself not deaf, was at least a fluent, and preferably native, user of Sign.

10. Victor, the Wild Boy, was first seen in the woods of Aveyron in 1799, going on all fours, eating acorns, leading an animal's life. When he was brought to Paris in 1800, he aroused enormous philosophical and pedagogical interest: How did he think? Could he be educated? The physician Jean-Marc Itard, also notable for his understanding (and his misunderstandings) of the deaf, took the boy into his house and tried to teach him language and educate him. Itard's first memoir was published in 1807 and was followed by many others. Harlan Lane has also devoted a book to him, which meditates, among other things, on the contrast between such "wild" boys and those born deaf.

Eighteenth-century romantic thought, of which Rousseau was so notable an example, was disposed to see all inequality, all misery, all guilt, all constraint as due to civilization, and to feel that innocence and freedom could only be found in Nature: "Man is born free, but is everywhere in chains." The horrifying reality of Victor was something of a corrective to this, a revelation that, as Clifford Geertz puts it:

> there is no such thing as a human nature independent of culture. Men without culture would not be . . . the nature's noblemen of Enlightenment primitivism. . . . They would be unworkable monstrosities with very few useful instincts, fewer recognizable sentiments, and no intellect: mental basket cases. . . . As our central nervous system—and most particularly its crowning curse and glory, the neocortex—grew up in great part in interaction with culture, it is incapable of directing our behavior or organizing our experience without the guidance provided by systems of significant symbols. . . . We are, in sum, incomplete or unfinished animals who complete or finish ourselves through culture (Geertz, 1973, p. 49).

11. Miller, 1976.

12. As early as the sixteenth century some of the deaf children of noble families had been taught to speak and read, through many years of tutoring, so that they could be recognized as persons under the law (mutes were not recognized) and could inherit their families' titles and fortunes. Pedro Ponce de Léon in sixteenth-century Spain, the Braidwoods in Britain, Amman in Holland, and Pereire and Deschamps in France were all hearing educators who achieved greater or lesser success in teaching some deaf persons to speak. Lane stresses that many of these educators depended upon signs and finger spelling to teach speech. Indeed, even the most celebrated of these oral deaf pupils knew and used sign language. Their speech was usually poorly intelligible and tended to regress as soon as intensive tutoring was curtailed. But before 1750, for the generality, for 99.9 percent of those born deaf, there was no hope of literacy or education.

13. There have been, however, purely written languages, such as the scholarly language used for over a thousand years by the elite Chinese

bureaucracy, which was never spoken and, indeed, never intended to be spoken.

14. De l'Epée exactly echoes his contemporary Rousseau, as do all the eighteenth-century descriptions of Sign. Rousseau (in his *Discourse on the Origin of Inequality* and his *Essay on the Origin of Language*) conceives of a primordial or original human language, in which everything has its true and natural name; a language so concrete, so particular, that it can catch the essence, the "itness," of everything; so spontaneous that it expresses all emotion directly, and so transparent that it is incapable of any evasion or deception. Such a language would be without (and indeed would have no need for) logic, grammar, metaphor, or abstractions—it would be a language not mediate, a symbolic expression of thought and feeling, but, almost magically, an *im*mediate one. Perhaps the thought of such a language—a language of the heart, a language of perfect transparency and lucidity, a language that can say everything, without ever deceiving or entangling us (Wittgenstein often spoke of the bewitchment of language), a language as pure and profound as music—is a universal fantasy.

15. This notion that sign language is uniform and universal, and enables deaf people all over the world to communicate with one another instantly, is still quite widespread. It is quite untrue. There are hundreds of different signed languages that have arisen independently wherever there are significant numbers of deaf people in contact. Thus there is American Sign Language, British Sign Language, French Sign Language, Danish Sign Language, Chinese Sign Language, and Mayan Sign Language, although these have no relation to spoken English, French, Chinese, etc. (More than fifty native sign languages, from Australian aboriginal to Yugoslavian, are described in detail in the *Gallaudet Encyclopedia of Deaf People and Deafness*, edited by John Van Cleve.)

16. Hughlings-Jackson's writings on language and aphasia are conveniently brought together in a volume of *Brain* published in 1915, shortly after his death. The best critique of the Jacksonian notion of "propositionizing" is to be found in Chapter III of Henry Head's wonderful two volumes, *Aphasia and Kindred Disorders of Speech*.

17. It was indeed his ignorance or incredulity in this that led him to propose, and impose, his entirely superfluous, indeed absurd, system of "Methodical Signs," which to some extent retarded the education and communication of the deaf. De l'Epée's apprehension of sign language was both exalted and depreciated. He saw it, on the one hand, as a "universal" language; on the other, as having no grammar (and thus in need of the importation of French grammar, for example). This mis-apprehension persisted for sixty years, until Roch-Ambroise Bébian, Sicard's pupil, seeing clearly that the indigenous sign language was autonomous and complete, threw the "methodical signs," the imported grammar, out.

18. In *When the Mind Hears*, Harlan Lane becomes a novelist-biographer-historian and assumes the persona of Clerc, through whom he recounts the early history of the deaf. Since Clerc's rich and long life spanned the most crucial developments, in many of which, indeed, he played a leading part, his "autobiography" becomes a won-derfully personal history of the deaf.

The story of Laurent Clerc's enlistment and coming to America is a cherished piece of deaf history and folklore. As the Reverend Thomas Gallaudet (so the story goes) was watching some children playing in his garden one day, he was struck by the fact that one of them did not join in the fun. He found out that her name was Alice Cogswell—and that she was deaf. He tried to teach her himself and then spoke to her father, Mason Cogswell, a surgeon in Hartford, about setting up a school for the deaf there (there were no schools for the deaf in the United States at this time).

Gallaudet sailed for Europe, looking for a teacher, someone who could found, or help found, a school in Hartford. He went first to England, to one of the Braidwood schools, one of the "oral" schools that had been set up in the previous century (it was a Braidwood school that Samuel Johnson had seen, on his journey to the Hebrides), but was given a cold welcome there: the oral method, he was told, was a "secret." After this experience in England, he went on to Paris, and there found Laurent Clerc teaching in the Institute of Deaf-Mutes. Would *he*—himself a deaf-mute, who had never ventured from his native France; nor indeed, much beyond the confines of the Insti-tute—would he be willing to come and bring the Word (the Sign) to

America? Clerc agreed, and the two of them set sail; and on the fifty-two-day journey to the United States, he taught Gallaudet Sign, and Gallaudet taught him English. Soon after their arrival, they started raising funds—both public and legislature were excited and generous—and the next year, with Mason Cogswell, they opened the Asylum in Hartford. A statue of Thomas Gallaudet, giving a lesson to Alice, stands on the grounds of Gallaudet University today.

19. This atmosphere breathes from every page of a delightful book, *The Deaf and the Dumb* by Edwin John Mann, Late Pupil of the Hartford Asylum, published by Hitchcock in 1836.

20. We lack sufficient direct knowledge of the evolution of ASL, especially in its first fifty years, when a far-reaching "creolization" occurred, as French Sign Language became Americanized (see Fischer, 1978, and Woodward, 1978).There was already a wide gulf between French Sign and the new creole ASL by 1867—Clerc himself commented on this—and this has continued to grow in the past hundred and twenty years. Nonetheless, there are still significant similarities between the two languages—sufficient for an American signer to feel somewhat at home in Paris. In contrast, American signers have great difficulty understanding British Sign Language, which has quite different indigenous origins of its own.

21. Indigenous sign dialects may be extremely different: thus prior to 1817, a deaf American traveling across the States would encounter sign dialects incomprehensibly different from his own; and standardization was so slow in England that until quite recently signers in adjacent villages might be mutually unintelligible.

22. The old terms "deaf and dumb" and "deaf-mute" referred to a supposed inadequacy of those born deaf to speak. They are, of course, perfectly capable of speech—they have the same speech apparatus as anyone else; what they lack is the ability to hear their own speech, and thus to monitor its sound by ear. Their speech, therefore, may be abnormal in amplitude and tone, with many omitted consonants and other speech sounds, sometimes so much so as to be unintelligible. Since deaf people cannot monitor their speech by ear, they have to

learn to monitor it by other senses—by vision, touch, vibration-sense, and kinesthesia. Moreover, the prelingually deaf have no auditory image, no *idea* what speech actually sounds like, no idea of a sound-meaning correspondence. What is essentially an auditory phenomenon must be grasped and controlled by nonauditory means. It is this which poses great difficulties, and which may require thousands of hours of individual tuition to achieve.

It is for this reason that the voices of the pre- and postlingually deaf are usually quite different, and distinguishable at once; the postlingually deaf *remember* how to speak, even though they can no longer readily monitor their speech; the prelingually deaf must be *taught* how to speak, without any sense or memory of how it sounds.

23. Although Bell has been seen as something of an ogre by the deaf (George Veditz, a former president of the National Association of the Deaf, and a hero of the deaf, called him "the most to be feared enemy of the American deaf"), it should be noted that Bell said on one occasion:

> I think that if we have the mental condition of the child alone in view without reference to language, no language will reach the mind like the language of signs; it is the method of reaching the mind of the deaf child.

Nor was he himself ignorant of Sign; he was, on the contrary, "a fluent signer on his fingers—as good as any deaf-mute . . . [he] could use his fingers with bewitching grace and ease," in the words of his deaf friend Albert Ballin. Ballin also called Bell's interest in the deaf "a hobby"—but it bears many of the marks, rather, of a violent and conflicted obsession (see Gannon, 1981, pp. 78–79).

24. Many of the deaf are now functional illiterates. A study carried out by Gallaudet College in 1972 showed that the average reading level of eighteen-year-old deaf high school graduates in the United States was only at a fourth-grade level, and a study by the British psychologist R. Conrad indicates a similar situation in England, with deaf students, at graduation, reading at the level of nine-year-olds (Conrad, 1979).

25. There had, of course, been other novels, like Carson McCullers's *The Heart Is a Lonely Hunter.* The figure of Mr. Singer, an isolated deaf

man in a hearing world, in this book is quite different from the protagonists of Greenberg's novel, who are vividly conscious of their
deaf identities. A huge social change, a change in social outlook, has
occurred in the intervening thirty years, with above all, the emergence
of a new self-consciousness.

26. Though there may be early development of a vocabulary of signs,
the development of Sign grammar takes place at the same age, and in
the same way, as the acquisition of speech grammar. Linguistic development thus occurs at the same rate in all children, deaf or hearing. If
signs appear earlier than speech, it is because they are easier to make,
for they involve relatively simple and slow movements of muscles,
whereas speech involves the lightning coordination of hundreds of
different structures, and only becomes possible in the second year of
life. Yet it is intriguing that a deaf child at four months may make the
sign for "milk," where a hearing child can only cry or look around.
Perhaps all babies would be better off knowing a few signs!

27. One may suspect deafness from observation, but one cannot easily
prove it in the first year of life. If, therefore, there is any reason to suspect deafness—for example, because there have been other deaf people
in the family, or there is a lack of response to sudden noises—there
should be physiological testing of the brain's response to sound (measuring so-called auditory evoked potentials in the brainstem). This
test, relatively simple, can confirm or rule out the diagnosis of deafness as early as the first week of life.

28. Sicard imagined such a community:

Could there not be in some corner of the world a whole society of
deaf people? Well then! Would we think that these individuals
were inferior, that they were unintelligent and lacked communication? They would certainly have a sign language, perhaps a language even richer than ours. This language would at least be
unambiguous, always giving an accurate picture of the mind's
affections. So why would this people be uncivilized? Why wouldn't
they in fact have laws, government, police less mistrustful than our
own? (Lane, 1984b, pp. 89–90).

This vision, so idyllic for Sicard, is also imagined—but as horrific—by the equally hyperbolic Alexander Graham Bell, whose fear-filled 1883 *Memoir upon the Formation of a Deaf Variety of the Human Race*, with its draconian suggestions for "dealing with" the deaf, was prompted by his experience on Martha's Vineyard (see below). There is a hint of both feelings—the idyllic and the horrific—in H. G. Wells's great tale "The Country of the Blind."

The deaf themselves have had occasional impulses to deaf separatism or deaf "Zionism." In 1831 Edmund Booth suggested the formation of a deaf township or community, and in 1856 John James Flournoy the establishment of a deaf state, "out west." And in fantasy the idea is still active. Thus Lyson C. Sulla, the deaf hero of *Islay*, dreams of becoming governor of the state of Islay and making it a state "of, by, and for" deaf people (Bullard, 1986).

29. There have been and are other isolated communities with a high incidence of deafness and unusually benign social attitudes to the deaf and their language. This is the case on Providence Island in the Caribbean, which has been studied in great detail by James Woodward (1982), and is also described by William Washabaugh.

Perhaps the Martha's Vineyard example is not that rare; perhaps it may indeed be expected to occur whenever there are significant numbers of deaf people in a community. There is an isolated village in the Yucatán (discovered and originally filmed by ethnographer and filmmaker Hubert Smith, and now being studied linguistically and anthropologically by Robert Johnson and Jane Norman of Gallaudet University) where thirteen adults, and one baby, out of a population of about 400, are congenitally deaf—here again the whole village uses Sign. There are other deaf relatives—cousins, second cousins, etc.—in nearby villages.

The Sign they use is not "home sign," but a Mayan Sign that is clearly of some antiquity, because it is intelligible to all of these deaf people, even though they are scattered over hundreds of square miles, and have virtually no contact with each other. This is quite different from the Central Mexican Sign used in Merida and other cities—indeed, they are mutually unintelligible. The well-integrated, full lives of the rural deaf—in communities that accept them wholly, and have adapted by themselves learning Sign—is in great contrast to the low social, informational, educational, and linguistic level of the "city" deaf in Merida, who find themselves fit (after years of inadequate schooling) only for peddling or perhaps riding bike-taxis. One sees here how well the community often works, while the "system" does badly.

30. Besides its exemplary school for the deaf, the town of Fremont, California, offers unrivaled work opportunities for deaf people, as well as a rare degree of public and civic awareness and respect. The existence of thousands of deaf people in one area of Fremont has given rise to a fascinating bilingual and bicultural situation, whereby speech and Sign are used equally. In certain parts of town, one may see cafes where half the customers speak and half sign, Y's where deaf and hearing work out together, and athletic matches where deaf and hearing play together. There is here not only an interface—and a friendly one, between deaf and hearing—but a considerable fusion or diffusion of the two cultures, so that numbers of the hearing (especially children) have started to acquire Sign, usually quite unconsciously, by picking it up rather than deliberately learning it. Thus even here, in a bustling industrial Silicon Valley town in the 1980s (and there is a somewhat similar situation in Rochester, New York, where several thousand deaf students, some with deaf families, attend the NTID), we see that the benign Martha's Vineyard situation can re-emerge.

31. I recently met a young woman, Deborah H., the hearing child of deaf parents, and a native signer herself, who tells me that she often falls back into Sign, and "thinks in Sign," whenever she has to puzzle out a complex intellectual problem. Language has an intellectual no less than a social function, and for Deborah, who hears, and lives now in a hearing world, the social function, very naturally, goes with speech, but the intellectual function, apparently, is still vested for her in Sign.

Addendum (1990): An interesting dissociation or doubleness of verbal and motor expression is reported by Arlow (1976) in a psychoanalytic study of a hearing child of deaf parents:

> Communication by motor behaviour became a very important part of the transference. . . . [W]ithout knowing it, I was receiving two sets of communication simultaneously: one in words, a form in which the patient ordinarily communicated with me; the

other in gestures [signs], as the patient used to communicate with his father. At other times in the transference, the motor symbols represented a gloss upon the verbal text the patient was communicating. These motor symbols contained additional material which either augmented or more likely contradicted what was being communicated verbally. In a sense, "unconscious material" was making its appearance in consciousness by way of motor rather than by way of verbal communication.

Part II: Thinking in Sign

1. It is all too common for deafness not to be noticed in infancy, even by intelligent and otherwise observant parents, and for it only to be diagnosed belatedly when the child fails to develop speech. The additional diagnosis of "dumb" or "retarded" is also too common and may remain throughout life. Many large "mental" hospitals and institutions tend to house a number of congenitally deaf patients called "retarded" or "withdrawn" or "autistic" who may not be any of these, but have been treated as such, and deprived of a normal development, from their earliest days.

2. Or is he? William James, always interested in the relation of thought to language, corresponded with Theophilus d'Estrella, a gifted deaf artist and photographer, and in 1893 published an autobiographical letter from d'Estrella to him, along with his own reflections on it. D'Estrella was born deaf, and did not start to acquire any formal sign language until he was nine (though he had devised a fluent "home-sign" from earliest childhood). At first, he writes:

> I thought in pictures and signs before I came to school. The pictures were not exact in detail, but were general. They were momentary and fleeting in my mind's eyes. The [home] signs were not extensive but somewhat conventional [pictorial] after the Mexican style ... not at all like the symbols of the deaf and dumb language.

Languageless though he was, d'Estrella was clearly inquisitive, imaginative, and thoughtful, even speculative, as a child: he thinks the

briny sea is the urine of a great Sea-God, and the moon a goddess in
the sky. All this he was able to relate when, in his tenth year, he started
at the California School for the Deaf, and learned to sign and write.
D'Estrella considered that he *did* think, that he thought widely, albeit
in images and pictures, before he acquired formal language; that language served to "elaborate" his thoughts without being necessary for
thought in the first place. This too was James' conclusion:

> His cosmological and ethical reflections were the outbirth of his
> solitary thought. . . . He surely had no conventional gestures for
> the casual and logical relations involved in his inductions about
> the moon, for example. So far as it goes then, *his narrative tends to
> discountenance the notion that no abstract thought is possible without
> words.* Abstract thought of a decidedly subtle kind, both scientific
> and moral, went on here in advance of the means of expressing it
> to others. [Emphasis added.]

James felt that the study of such deaf people could be of major importance in casting light on the relation of thought to language. (It
should be added that doubt was expressed by some of James's critics
and correspondents about the reliability of d'Estrella's autobiographical account.)

But *is* thought, all thought, dependent upon language? It would
certainly seem, if introspective accounts can be trusted, that mathematical thought (perhaps a very special form of thought) can proceed
in its absence. Roger Penrose, the mathematician, discusses this at
some length (Penrose, 1989) and gives examples from his own intro-
spection, as well as from autobiographical accounts by Poincaré, Einstein, Galton, and others. Einstein, when asked about his own
thinking, wrote:

> The words or the language as they are written or spoken, do not
> seem to play any role in my mechanism of thought. The psychi-
> cal entities which seem to serve as elements of thought are cer-
> tain *signs*, and more or less clear *images* . . . of visual and some
> muscular type. Conventional words or other signs have to be
> sought for laboriously only in a second stage.

And Jacques Hadamard, in *The Psychology of Mathematical Invention*,
writes:

> I insist that words are totally absent from my mind when I really think . . . [and] even after reading or hearing a question, every word disappears the moment that I am beginning to think it over; and I fully agree with Schopenhauer when he writes "thoughts die the moment they are embodied by words."

Penrose, who is himself a geometer, concludes that words are almost useless for mathematical thinking, even though they might be well suited for other sorts of thinking. No doubt a chess player, or a computer programmer, or a musician, or an actor, or a visual artist would come to somewhat similar conclusions. It is clear that language, as narrowly conceived, is not the only vehicle or tool for thought. Perhaps we need to enlarge the domain of "language," so that it embraces mathematics, music, acting, art . . . *every* form of representational system.

But does one actually *think* in these? Did Beethoven, late Beethoven, actually think in music? It seems unlikely, even though his thought was articulated, and issued, in music, and cannot be glimpsed or grasped except *through* it. (He was at all times a great formalist, and by this time had been deaf, and auditorily deafferented, for twenty years.) Did Newton think in differential equations when he was "voyaging through strange seas of thought, alone"? This too seems unlikely, but his thought can scarcely be grasped except *through* the equations. One does not think, at the deepest level, in music or equations, nor, perhaps even for verbal artists, in language either. Schopenhauer and Vygotsky are both great verbal artists, whose thought, it might seem, is inseparable from their words; but both insist it is beyond words: "Thoughts die," Schopenhauer writes, "the moment they are embodied by words." "Words die," Vygotsky writes, "as they bring forth thought."

But if thought transcends language, and all representational forms, nonetheless it creates these, and needs these, for its advancement. It did so in human history, and does so in each of us. Thought is not language, or symbolism, or imagery, or music—but without these it may die, stillborn, in the head. It is this which threatens a Joseph, a d'Estrella, a Massieu, an Ildefonso; which threatens any deaf child, or any child whatever, not given full access to language and other cultural tools and forms.

3. A. R. Luria and F. Ia. Yudovich describe identical twins with a congenital language retardation (due to cerebral problems, not to deafness). These twins, although of normal intelligence, and even bright, functioned in a very primitive way—their play was repetitive and uncreative. They had extreme difficulty thinking out problems, conceiving complex actions or plans; there was, in Luria's words, "a peculiar, insufficiently differentiated, structure of consciousness, [with inability] to detach word from action, to master orienting, to plan activity . . . to formulate the aims of activity with the aid of speech."

When the twins were separated, and each acquired a normal language system, "the whole structure of the mental life of both twins was simultaneously and sharply changed . . . and after only three months we observed the beginnings of meaningful play . . . the possibility of productive, constructive activity in the light of formulated aims . . . intellectual operations which shortly before this were only in an embryonic state. . . ."

All of these "cardinal improvements" (as Luria puts it), improvements not only in intellectual functioning but in the entire being of the children, "we could only attribute to the influence of the one changed factor—the acquisition of a language system."

Luria and Yudovich also comment about the disabilities of the languageless deaf:

The deaf mute who has not been taught to speak . . . does not possess all those forms of reflection which are realized through speech. . . . [He] indicates objects or actions with a gesture; he is unable to form abstract concepts, to systematize the phenomena of the external world with the aid of abstracted signals furnished by language but which are not natural to visual, practically acquired experience.

One must regret that Luria, apparently, had no experience with deaf people who had acquired fluent language, for he would have provided us with incomparable descriptions of the acquisition of conceptual and systematizing power *with* language.

Addendum (1990): I have recently learned that, although he never published on the subject, Luria *did* have a great deal to do during the 1950s, with deaf (and deaf-blind) children, and the role of sign language in their education and development. This represented, in a way, a return to the "defectology" which he and Vygotsky had pioneered in the 1920s and 1930s, and which he was later to explore in his rehabilitative approaches to the neurologically injured.

4. *Note 1990:* Recently, while in Italy, I encountered a nine-year-old gypsy boy, Manuel, who had been born deaf, but had never met other deaf people, and (with his itinerant life) had never received any education. He was quite languageless, with neither Sign nor Italian, but bright, affectionate, and emotionally normal—he was much loved by his parents and older siblings, and entrusted by them with all sorts of tasks. When he entered the via Nomentana school for the deaf, there was doubt as to whether he would acquire language fluently at his age. But he has done brilliantly, and in three months has already acquired fair Sign and fair Italian, loves both languages, loves communicating, and is full of questions and curiosity and intellectual vitality. He has done much better than poor Joseph, whose acquisition of language has been slow and laborious.

Why the difference? Manuel is clearly a very bright child indeed, and Joseph one of ordinary (though not subnormal) intelligence; but, perhaps more to the point, Manuel was always loved, always involved, always *treated as normal*—he was completely a part of his family and community, who saw him as different but never as alien— whereas Joseph was regarded, and often treated, as autistic or retarded. Manuel was never left out, never *felt* left out; he did not suffer, as Joseph did, from an annihilating sense of left-outness and isolation.

This emotional factor is probably of great importance in determining whether or not language acquisition will be successful near or after the "critical age." Thus Ildefonso was successful, but three other languageless deaf adults whom Susan Schaller encountered had been so damaged emotionally by isolation (and in one case institutionalization as well) that they had become withdrawn and inaccessible, *had turned against communication*, and were no longer open to any attempts to establish formal language.

5. Massieu's autobiography is reprinted in Harlan Lane's *The Deaf Experience*, pp. 76–80, and Sicard's book is also excerpted here, pp. 83–126.

6. In 1977 S. Goldin-Meadow and H. Feldman began videotaping a group of profoundly deaf preschool children who were isolated from other signers, because their parents preferred them to learn speech and lip-reading. Despite this isolation, and their parents' strong encouragement to use speech, the children began to create gestures—first single gestures, then strings of gestures—to represent people, objects, and actions. This is what happened with Massieu and others in the eighteenth century. The "home signs" that Massieu developed, and that these isolated preschool children developed, are simple gestural systems that may have a rudimentary syntax and morphology of a very limited sort; but they do not make the transition, the leap into a full grammar and syntax, such as occurs when a child is exposed to Sign.

Similar observations have been made of isolated deaf adults—there was one such deaf man in the Solomon Islands, the first in twenty-four generations (Kuschel, 1973); they too will invent gestural systems, with a very simple syntax and morphology, by which they can communicate basic needs and feelings to their neighbors—but cannot *by themselves* make the qualitative leap from such a gestural system into a complete, fully grammaticized linguistic system.

We see here, as Carol Padden and Tom Humphries point out, poignant attempts to invent a language within one lifetime. And, essentially, this cannot be done, because it requires a child, and a child's brain, exposed to a natural language, to create and transmit, to evolve, a natural language. Thus sign languages are *historical* creations that require, at the very least, two generations, for their genesis. Sign may become still richer, evolve, with several generations, as was the case on Martha's Vineyard, but two generations are *enough*.

We see the same situation with speech. Thus when linguistically different communities meet and have to communicate, they develop an improvised, grammarless pidgin. Grammar only appears in the next generation, when the children bring it to their parents' pidgin, creating a rich and fully grammaticized creole. This at least is the thesis of the linguist Derek Bickerton (see Restak, 1988, pp. 216–217). Thus, a deaf Adam and Eve would improvise signs but lack language; a true, grammatical sign language would evolve only with the development of their children, Cain and Abel.

It seems clear that grammatical potential is present, even explosively present, in every child's brain, and that it will leap out and actualize itself given the least opportunity. This is particularly clear in the case of deaf children who have been isolated, but who are finally, serendipitously, exposed to Sign. In this instance, even the briefest exposure to a fully grammaticized sign language can serve to initiate a huge and rapidly spreading change. A glimpse of a subject/object usage, or a sentence construction, may ignite the latent grammatical power of the brain and produce a sudden fulguration, and a very rapid conversion from a gestural system to a true language. Grammar can spread, among such children, like a contagion. It must take a very exceptional degree of isolation, indeed, to prevent this happening.

7. Massieu's enthralled naming of trees and other plants helped to define them in unique *perceptual* categories ("this is an oak, this is 'oak-ishness'!"), but not to define them in a more *conceptual* way ("Ha, a gymnosperm!" or "Ha, another crucifer!"). And many of these "natural" categories, of course, were already familiar to him. There was much more difficulty with unfamiliar objects, which had not previously been part of the perceptual world. This is hinted at in Massieu, and absolutely clear with the Wild Boy, Victor. Thus when Itard, Victor's teacher, taught him the word "book," this was first taken to refer to a *particular* book, and the same failure occurred with other words, all of which he understood to name some particular thing, not a category of things. Sicard introduced Massieu, at first, to images, and thence conducted him to (what Lévy-Bruhl, in his studies of primitive thinking, calls) "image-concepts." Such concepts are necessarily particular, because one cannot have a generic image.

8. L. S. Vygotsky was born in Byelorussia in 1896, and as a very young man published a remarkable book on the psychology of art. He then turned to systematic psychology, and in the ten years before his death (from tuberculosis, at the age of 38) produced a unique corpus of work, which was seen by most of his contemporaries (including Piaget) as showing outstanding originality, indeed genius. Vygotsky saw the development of language and mental powers as neither learned, in the ordinary way, nor emerging epigenetically, but as being social and mediate in nature, as arising from the interaction of adult and child, and as internalizing the cultural instrument of language for the processes of thought.

His work aroused great suspicion among Marxist ideologues, and *Thought and Language*, which was published posthumously in 1934, was banned and suppressed a couple of years later, as "anti-Marxist," "anti-Pavlovian," and "anti-Soviet." His work and theories could no longer be mentioned publicly, but were treasured by his pupils and colleagues—A. R. Luria and A. N. Leont'ev, above all. In later life, Luria wrote that meeting a genius such as Vygotsky, and getting to know him, was the most crucial event of his life—and he often saw his own work as "nothing more than a continuation" of Vygotsky's. It was largely through Luria's courageous efforts (for he too had been banned and forced into "internal exile" at different periods) that *Thought and Language* was republished (in Russian and German) in the late 1950s.

It was published in English, finally, in 1962, with an introduction by Jerome Bruner. It decisively influenced Bruner's own work—his books of the 1960s (most notably *Towards a Theory of Instruction*) are powerfully Vygotskian in tone. Vygotsky's work was so ahead of its time in the 1930s that one of his contemporaries described him as "a visitor from the future." But in the past twenty years he has provided, increasingly, the theoretical underpinning for a variety of important studies on the development of language and mental processes (and thus the education) of the child, including those of Schlesinger and the Woods, which focus on deaf children. It is only now, in the late 1980s, that Vygotsky's collected works are being made available in English, again under the general editorship of Bruner.

Addendum (1990): It is only now that Vygotsky's collected essays on "Defectology," including his crucial 1925 essay on special education for the deaf, are published in English (see Vygotsky, 1991 and Knox, 1989). "Defectology," it must be said first, is not only a hideous word, but a misleading one, for it is not defects that it is concerned with, but the very opposite—adaptations, compensations (perhaps indeed it should be called "intactology"). Vygotsky was passionately opposed to the evaluation of handicapped children in terms of their defects or deficits, their "minuses"; he valued them instead for their intactnesses, their "pluses." He did not see them as defective, but different: "A handicapped child represents a qualitatively different, unique type of development." And it was this qualitative difference, this uniqueness, Vygotsky felt, that any educational or rehabilitative enterprise must

address: "If a blind or deaf child achieves the same level of development as a normal child," he writes, "then the child with a defect
achieves this *in another way, by another course, by other means;* and, for the
pedagogue, it is particularly important to know the uniqueness of the
course along which he must lead the child. This uniqueness transforms the minus of the handicap into the plus of compensation."

Development of higher psychological functions, for Vygotsky, is not
something which occurs "naturally," automatically—it requires media-
tion, culture, a cultural tool. And the most important such cultural tool
is language. But cultural tools and languages, he argues, have been
developed for the "normal" person, the person with all his sense organs,
his biological functions, intact. What then will be best for the handicapped, the *different* person? The key to his development will be compensation—the use of an alternative cultural tool. Thus Vygotsky
comes to the special education of the deaf: the alternative cultural tool,
for them, is sign language—sign language which has been created for
them and by them. Sign language addresses the functions, the visual
functions, that are still intact; it is the most direct way of reaching deaf
children, the simplest means of allowing their full development, and
the only one that respects their difference, their uniqueness.

9. Kaspar Hauser, after his release from years of languagelessness in a
dungeon (described later in this chapter) showed an identical tendency
to use such metaphors at first, toward a sort of natural, naïf, childlike
poetry . . . which his teacher, von Feuerbach, demanded he "abandon."
One sees in the history and evolution of many peoples and cultures
such a "primitive" poetic language at first, subsequently displaced by
more analytic, abstract terms. One sometimes feels that the loss may
be as great as the gain.

Lévy-Bruhl, similarly, describes how the Tasmanians "had no
words to represent abstract ideas . . . could not express qualities such
as hard, soft, round, tall, short, etc. To signify hard they would say, like
a stone; for tall, big legs; round, like a ball; like the moon; and so on,
always combining their words with gestures, designed to bring what
they were describing before the eyes of the person addressed." One is
irresistibly reminded here of Massieu as he learned language—of how
he would say, "Albert is bird," "Paul is lion," before he acquired, or
turned to, the use of generic adjectives.

10. Massieu's acquiring the *idea* of a square, through the medium of a common word, a symbol for it, was (consciously and unconsciously) Sicard's answer to Hobbes. For Hobbes had argued, a century and a half earlier, that though a deaf person might work out that the angles of a triangle were the sum of two right angles, and even follow Euclid's proof of this, he could not conceive this as a universal proposition about triangles, because he lacked a word or symbol for "triangle." Lacking common nouns, lacking abstract language, Hobbes thought, the deaf could not generalize. Perhaps, said Sicard; but if they use common nouns, use abstract language, use sign language, they can generalize as well as anyone else. One is reminded, as one reads Sicard, of Plato's theory of ideas and education, especially in the *Cratylus* and *Meno*. First, says Plato, one must see actual chairs or squares—all sorts of objects with squareness (or any other quality)—only then can the idea of squareness come, the archetypal or ideal square of which all squares are merely copies. In the *Meno* an ignorant and illiterate youth, with no idea of geometry, is gradually inducted into the truths of geometry, gradually drawn to higher and higher levels of abstraction, through the questions of a teacher who is always a stage ahead and who, by the form of his question, allows the pupil to advance to his stage. Thus, for Plato, language, knowledge, epistemology, is innate—all learning is essentially "reminiscence"—but this can only occur with another, a mediator, in the context of a dialogue. Sicard, a born teacher, was not really *instructing* Massieu; he was drawing him out, *educing* him, by means of such a dialogue.

11. Anselm von Feuerbach's original account was published in 1832, and translated into English—as *Caspar Hauser*—in 1834. It has been the subject of innumerable essays, articles, books; of a film by Werner Herzog; and of a remarkable psychoanalytic essay, by Leonard Shengold, in *Halo in the Sky*.

12. But then again, this may sometimes not happen. A modern day wild child, Genie, was found in California in 1970; she had been imprisoned at home (by her psychotic father) and not spoken to since infancy (see Curtiss, 1977). Despite the most intensive training, Genie acquired only a little language—a number of words for common objects, but no ability to ask questions and only the most rudimentary

grammar. Why did Kaspar do so well, and Genie so badly? It may have been, simply, that Kaspar had already acquired some language, the linguistic competence of a three-year-old, before he was locked up, whereas Genie had been totally isolated since the age of twenty months. This one year of language, indeed, can make all the difference: one sees this with children who have been suddenly deafened at, say, thirty-six months rather than twenty-four months.

13. In January 1982, a New York State court awarded $2.5 million to "a seventeen-year-old deaf boy who had been diagnosed an 'imbecile' at two years of age and put into an institution for the mentally retarded until he was almost eleven years old. At that age he was transferred to another institution, where a routine psychological examination revealed he was 'at least of normal intelligence.'" This is reported by Jerome D. Schein (Schein, 1984). Such cases may indeed be far from uncommon—an almost identical one is reported in *The New York Times* of December 11, 1988 (p. 81).

Addendum (1990): Such mistakes, incredibly, can happen in adult life too. Very recently, at a psychiatric hospital where I work, I saw a man who had become deaf at the age of thirty-eight, from an attack of meningitis. Suddenly he had found himself unable to hear, unable to understand what others were saying to him. He saw several physicians, none of whom, apparently, really took the time to listen to him or appreciate his situation. He was diagnosed as schizophrenic by one of them, as retarded by another. When I spent a little time with him, and wrote my questions out for him, it became obvious that he was neither—and that he did not need to be institutionalized but rather to be in school.

14. When I came to write of a set of twins who were calculating prodigies ("The Twins" in Sacks, 1985), and their extraordinary facility for numbers, their "numeracy," I had to wonder whether there might not be in their brains "a deep arithmetic of the kind described by Gauss . . . as innate as Chomsky's deep syntax and generative grammar." When I heard of Ildefonso's sudden understanding of numbers, his sudden "seeing" of arithmetical rules, I could not help thinking of the twins, and wondering whether he too was not possessed of an innate, organic arithmetic, suddenly kindled, or released, by a numerical stimulus.

Indeed, Schaller subsequently wrote to me about a fifty-four-year-old prelingually deaf man with no language, who did have, however, a good grasp of arithmetic and owned a much-cherished arithmetical primer which he could not read except for the actual arithmetical signs and examples. This man, twice Ildefonso's age, was able to acquire sign language in his sixth decade—Schaller wonders whether his arithmetical competence may have helped to make this possible.

Such an arithmetical competence might perhaps serve as a model, or primordium, for the development of a linguistic competence immediately (or long) afterward, one Chomskian power facilitating the emergence of another.

15. Rapin, 1979, p. 210.

16. St. Augustine writes:

> When they (my elders) named some object, and accordingly moved towards something, I saw this and I grasped that the thing was called by the sound they uttered when they meant to point it out. Their intention was shewn by their bodily movements, as it were the natural language of all peoples: the expression of the face, the play of the eyes, the movement of other parts of the body, and the tone of voice which expresses our state of mind in seeking, having, rejecting, or avoiding something. Thus, as I heard words repeatedly used in their proper places in various sentences, I gradually learnt to understand what objects they signified; and after I had trained my mouth to form these signs, I used them to express my own desires.
>
> —Confessions *I:8*

Wittgenstein remarks: "Augustine describes the learning of human language as if the child came into a strange country and did not understand the language of the country; that is, as if it already had a language, only not this one. Or again: as if the child could already *think*, only not yet speak. And 'think' would here mean something like 'talk to itself.'" (*Philosophical Investigations:* 32)

17. The cognitive aspects of such preverbal intercourse have been especially studied by Jerome Bruner and his colleagues (see Bruner, 1983). Bruner sees in preverbal interactions and "conversations" the

general pattern and archetype of all the verbal interactions, the dialogues, that will occur in the future. If these preverbal dialogues fail to occur, or go awry, Bruner feels, the stage is set for serious problems in later verbal intercourse. This, of course, is exactly what may happen—and does happen, if precautionary measures are not taken—with deaf infants, who cannot hear their mothers and who cannot hear the sound of her earliest preverbal communications.

David Wood, Heather Wood, Amanda Griffiths, and Ian Howarth, in their long-term study of deaf children, lay great emphasis on this. They write:

> Imagine a deaf baby with little or no awareness of sound.... When he looks at an object or event, he receives none of the "mood music" that accompanies the social experience of the hearing baby. Suppose he looks from an object of his attention to turn to an adult who is "sharing" the experience with him and the adult talks about what he has just been looking at. Does the infant even realize that *communication* is taking place? To discover the relationships between a word and its referent, the deaf infant has to *remember* something he has just observed and *relate* this memory to another observation.... The deaf baby has to do much more, "discovering" the relationships between two very different visual experiences that are displaced in time.

These and other major considerations, they feel, are liable to cause major communicative problems long before the development of language.

The deaf children of deaf parents have a fair chance of being spared these interactional difficulties, for their parents know all too well from their own experience that all communication, all play, all games must be visual, and in particular, "baby talk" must move into a visuo–gestural mode. Carol Erting and her colleagues have recently provided beautiful illustrations of the differences between deaf and hearing parents in this regard. In fact, an unusually visual, or hypervisual, orientation may be observed in deaf children almost from birth; and it is this, typically, which their parents, if deaf, recognize very early. Deaf children *from the start* show a different organization, and one which requires (as it demands) a different sort of response. Sensitive hearing parents may recognize this to some extent, and become quite skilled in visual interaction themselves. But there is a limit to what hearing parents, however loving, can provide; for they are, in their nature, auditory and not visual beings. A further, totally visual interaction is needed, if the deaf child is to develop his own special and unique identity—and this can only be conferred by another visual being, another deaf person.

18. Very detailed studies have also been carried out by Wood et al. in England, who, like Schlesinger, see the mediating role of parents and teachers as crucial and bring out how often, and in what various and subtle ways, this may be defective when dealing with deaf children.

19. Schlesinger, Hilde. "Buds of Development: Antecedents of Academic Achievement," work in progress.

20. This interplay is a major concern of cognitive psychology. See especially L. S. Vygotsky, *Thought and Language*; A. R. Luria and F. Ia. Yudovich, *Speech and the Development of Mental Processes in the Child*; and Jerome Bruner, *Child's Talk*. And, of course (and most especially with regard to the development of emotion, fantasy, creativity, and play) this is equally the concern of analytical psychology. See D. W. Winnicott, *The Maturational Process and the Facilitating Environment*; M. Mahler, F. Pine, and A. Bergman, *The Psychological Birth of the Human Infant*; and Daniel N. Stern, *The Interpersonal World of the Infant*.

21. Schlesinger, 1988, p. 262.

22. Eric Lenneberg feels that it is only in the *verbal* realm, after the age of three (say), that problems arise with the deaf; and in general, these are not severe in the preschool years. Thus he writes:

A healthy deaf child two years or older gets along famously despite his total inability to communicate verbally. These children become very clever in their pantomime and have well-developed techniques for communicating their desires, needs, and even their opinions. . . . The almost complete absence of language in these children is no hindrance to the most imaginative and intelligent play appropriate for the age. They love make-believe games; they can build fantastic structures with blocks or out of boxes; they may set up electric trains and develop the necessary logic for setting switches and anticipating the behavior of the moving train around curves and over bridges. They love to look at pictures, and no degree of stylizing renders the pictorial representation incomprehensible for them, and their own drawings leave nothing to be desired when compared with those produced by their hearing contemporaries. Thus, cognitive development as revealed through play seems to be no different from that which occurs in the presence of language development.

Lenneberg's view, which seemed reasonable in 1967, is not one that is now held by close observers of deaf children, all of whom feel that there may be major communicative and cognitive difficulties, even in preschool days, unless language is introduced as early as possible. Unless special measures are taken, the average deaf child will have only fifty to sixty words at the age of five or six, whereas the average hearing child has three thousand. Whatever the enchantments of toy trains and make-believe games, a child must be deprived of some aspects of childhood if he has, in effect, no language before going to school; there must be some communication with the parents, with other people, some understanding of the world in general, that is cut off. At least one would suspect so: we need careful studies, including perhaps analytic reconstructions, to see how the first five years of life are altered if one fails to acquire language during this period.

23. Schlesinger, Hilde. "Buds of Development: Antecedents of Academic Achievement," work in progress.

24. It does not matter *essentially*, Schlesinger believes, whether the dialogue between mother and child is in speech or Sign; what matters is its communicative intent. This intent—which, like so many intents, is largely unconscious—may be in the direction of trying to *control* the child, or in the healthy direction of fostering its growth, its autonomy, and its expansion of mind. But the use of Sign, other things being equal, clearly makes communication easier in very early life, because the deaf infant spontaneously picks up Sign, but cannot as readily pick up speech.

Schlesinger sees communicative intent as a function of "power"—whether the parents feel "powerful" or "powerless" in relation to their child. Powerful parents, in her formulation, feeling themselves autonomous and powerful, give autonomy and power to their children;

powerless ones, feeling themselves passive and controlled, in turn
exert an excessive control on their children, and monologue *at* them,
instead of having a dialogue *with* them. Having a deaf child, of course,
may give the parents a feeling of powerlessness: How can they communicate with the child? What can they do? What expectations can
they, or the child, have for the future? What sort of world will be
forced on them, or will they force on the child? What seems crucial is
that there be a feeling, not of force, but of choice—that there be a
desire for effective communication, whether it be speech, Sign, or both.

25. "For someone as deaf as Charlotte, lip-reading and intelligible
speech can be achieved only after years of hard work, if at all," writes
Sarah Elizabeth. This, at least, was her conclusion, after much study
and discussion. But the parents of another profoundly deaf little girl,
confronted with much the same situation, came to another conclusion,
and felt they had another option.

Alice was found to be profoundly deaf at the age of seventeen
months (with a hearing loss of 120 db in one ear and 108 db in the
other). One answer for her, her parents were persuaded, lay in Cued
Speech, coupled with the use of the most powerful hearing aids. (Cued
Speech, developed by Orin Cornett, makes use of simple hand positions about the mouth, which serve to clarify different sounds that
look alike to the lip reader.) Alice has apparently done well with this,
has acquired a large vocabulary and excellent grammar, and (at the
age of five) has an expressive language level twenty months in
advance of her age. She reads and writes well, *enjoys* reading and writing. She does well academically (she has a full-time Cued Speech interpreter at school). She is described by her parents as "very bright,
well-adjusted, popular, outgoing," though with some fears, now, about
finding herself "cut-off" in school.

But though her language abilities are so good, her ability to communicate has marked limitations. Her speech is still difficult to understand, has a "chopped-up quality," and leaves out many of the sounds
of spontaneous speech. She can be understood well by her parents and
teachers, but much less well by anyone else. She can clarify her meaning with expressive Cuing, but the number of people who understand
Cue is minimal. She is also somewhat below normal in her ability to
pick up speech: lip-reading is not just a visual skill—75 percent of it is

a sort of inspired guessing or hypothesizing, dependent on the use of contextual clues. It is easier for the postlingually deaf, who know speech, to "read" it; much more difficult for the prelingually deaf, like Alice. Thus, although she is in the hearing world, she faces great difficulties—and potential isolation—in it too. Life at home, before the age of five, with understanding parents, may not place too many demands upon a deaf child, but life thereafter is very different. The problems of a child with grossly defective speech and hearing are liable to increase dramatically with each year at school.

Alice's parents are open-minded, but did not force her exclusively toward Cuing; indeed, they were astonished that it worked. But they have clear preferences as to the world they would like their daughter to inhabit: "I want her to go either way," says her father, "but in my mind's eye I prefer to think of her in the hearing world, marrying a hearing person, etc. But she'd gain a tremendous amount of strength from another deaf person. . . . She loves signing too, she needs a relationship with another signer. I hope she can feel at home in *both* deaf and hearing worlds." One must hope that Alice can learn Sign, and now—because very soon it will be too late for her to acquire it with native competence. And if she does not acquire it, she may not find herself at home in *either* world.

26. It is certain that we are not "given" reality, but have to *construct* it for ourselves, in our own way, and that in doing so we are conditioned by the cultures and worlds we live in. It is natural that our language should embody our world view—the way in which we perceive and construct reality. But does it go further—does it *determine* our world view? This was the notorious hypothesis espoused by Benjamin Lee Whorf: that language comes before thought, and is the principal determinant of thought and reality. Whorf took his hypothesis to ultimate lengths: "A change in language can transform our appreciation of the cosmos" (thus, he felt, from contrasting their tense systems, that English speakers would be disposed to a Newtonian world view, but Hopi speakers to a relativistic and Einsteinian world view). His thesis gave rise to much misunderstanding and controversy, some of a frankly racist kind; but the evidence, as Roger Brown remarks, is "extraordinarily difficult to interpret," not least because we lack adequate independent definitions of thought and language.

But the difference between the most diverse spoken languages is small compared to the difference between speech and Sign. Sign differs in origins, and in biological mode. And this, in a way deeper than anything Whorf envisaged, may determine, or at least modify, the thought processes of those who sign, and give them a unique and untranslatable, hypervisual cognitive style.

27. I was reminded, when they said this, of an anecdote I had read about Ibsen: that once, when walking with a friend through a house they had never been in before, he turned suddenly and said, "What was in that room we just passed?" His friend had only the vaguest notion, but Ibsen gave a most exact description of everything in the room, its appearance, its location, its relation to everything else, and then said, under his breath, as if to himself, "I see everything."

28. Earlier concepts of grammar (as in the pedagogic Latin grammars that still torment schoolchildren) had been based on a mechanical, not a creative, concept of language. The Port-Royal *Grammar* saw grammar as essentially creative, speaking of "that marvelous invention by which we construct from twenty-five or thirty sounds an infinity of expressions, which, having no resemblance in themselves to what takes place in our minds, still enable us to let others know the secret of what we conceive and of all the varied mental activities we carry out."

29. Myklebust,1960.

30. One must wonder whether there is not also an intellectual (and almost physiological) difficulty here. It is not easy to imagine a grammar in space (or a grammaticization of space).This was not even a concept before Edward S. Klima and Ursula Bellugi conceived it, in 1970 (even to the deaf, who used such a grammar-space). Our extraordinary difficulty in even imagining a spatial grammar, a spatial syntax, a spatial language—imagining a linguistic use of space—may stem from the fact that "we" (the hearing, who do not sign), lacking any personal experience of grammaticizing space ourselves (and lacking, indeed, any cerebral substrate for it) are *physiologically* unable to imagine what it is like (any more than we can imagine having a tail or seeing infrared).

31. A particularly nice confirmation of Stokoe's insight is provided by "slips of the hand." These are never arbitrary errors, never movements or handshapes that do not occur in the language, but only errors of combination (transposition, etc.) in a limited set of place or movement or handshape parameters. They are entirely analogous to the phonemic errors that are involved in slips of the tongue.

Besides these errors (which involve unconscious transpositions of sublexical elements), there are among native signers elaborate forms of Sign wit and Art Sign, which involve conscious, creative plays on signs and their constituents. Such signers clearly have an intuitive awareness of the internal structure of signs.

Yet another (if offbeat) testament to the syntactic and phonemic structure of Sign comes from "mad Sign" or "Sign salad," which may be seen in states of schizophrenic psychosis. Here, typically, signs are split up, deconstituted, reconstituted, subject to neologistic formations and bizarre (but not "illegal") grammatical distortions. This is exactly what happens with spoken language in so-called "schizophrenese" or "word salad."

I have also seen an interesting isolation and exaggeration of different phonemic elements of signs (convulsive alteration of the location or direction of a sign, for example, while keeping the handshape constant; or vice versa) in a nine-year-old deaf girl who has Tourette's syndrome; similar strange emphases and distortions of spoken words may occur in hearing children who have Tourette's.

32. Stokoe's notation, it should be understood, was precisely this, a notation (like phonetic notation) for research purposes, not for ordinary use. (Some of the notations that have been proposed since are enormously complex: notation of a short sign phrase may occupy an entire page.) There has never been, in the ordinary sense, a written form of Sign, and some have doubted whether a written form would be practicable. As Stokoe remarks, "the Deaf may well sense that any effort to transcribe in two dimensions a language whose syntax uses the three dimensions of space as well as time would far outweigh the result—if it could be achieved" (personal communication; see also Stokoe, 1987).

Very recently, however, a new system of writing Sign—"Sign-Font"—*has* been developed by a group in San Diego (see Newkirk, 1987 and Hutchins et al., 1986). The use of computers makes it possible to give the immense range of signs, their modulations, and many of their "intonations" a more adequate written form than had previously been thought possible. SignFont tries to indicate the full expressiveness of Sign itself; it is too early to say, however, whether or not it will find favor in the deaf community.

If SignFont, or some other form of written Sign, were adopted by the deaf, it might lead them to a written literature of their own, and serve to deepen their sense of community and culture. This prospect, interestingly, was perceived by Alexander Graham Bell: "Another method of consolidating the deaf and dumb into a distinct class would be to reduce the sign-language to writing, so that the deaf-mutes would have a common literature distinct from the rest of the world." But this was seen by him in an entirely negative light, as predisposing towards "the formation of a deaf variety of the human race."

33. This was equally the case with Bernard Tervoort's remarkable thesis on Dutch Sign Language, published in Amsterdam in 1952. This important early work was totally ignored at the time.

34. Besides the immense number of grammatical modulations that signs can undergo (there are literally hundreds of these, for example, for the root sign LOOK), the actual vocabulary of Sign is far larger and richer than any existing dictionary represents. Sign languages are evolving almost explosively at this time (this is especially true of the newest ones, like Israeli Sign). There is a continual proliferation of neologisms: some of these represent borrowings from English (or whatever the surrounding spoken language), some are mimetic depictions, some are ad hoc inventions, but most are created by the remarkable range of formal devices available within the language itself. These have been especially studied by Ursula Bellugi and Don Newkirk.

35. Visual images are not mechanical, or passive, like photographic ones; they are, rather, analytical constructions. Elementary feature-detectors—for vertical lines, horizontal lines, angles, etc.—were first described by David Hubel and Torsten Wiesel. And at a higher level the image must be composed and structured with the aid of what Richard Gregory has called a "visual grammar" (see "The Grammar of Vision," in Gregory, 1974).

A question which has been raised by Bellugi and others is whether sign language has the *same* generative grammar as speech, the *same* deep neural and grammatical basis. Since the "deep structure" of language, as envisioned by Chomsky, has an essentially abstract or mathematical nature, it could, in principle, be mapped equally well onto the surface structure of a sign language, a touch language, a smell language, whatever. The modality of the language, as such, would not (necessarily) present any problem.

A more fundamental question, raised above all by Edelman, is whether *any* innate or rule-bound basis is needed for language development at all; whether the brain/mind might not proceed in a quite different fashion, *creating* the linguistic categories and relationships it needs, as (in Edelman's terms) it creates perceptual categories, without prior knowledge, in an "unlabelled" world (Edelman, 1990).

36. The question of whether some nonhuman species have language, languages that make "infinite use of finite means," remains a confused and contentious one. As a neurologist I have been intrigued by descriptions of aphasia in monkeys, which suggest that the neural primordia of language, at least, evolved before man (see Heffner and Heffner, 1988).

Chimpanzees are unable to speak (their vocal apparatus is geared only for relatively crude sounds), but are able to make *signs* quite well, to acquire a vocabulary of several hundred signs. In the case of pygmy chimpanzees, indeed, such signs (or "symbols") may be used spontaneously and passed on to other chimps. There is no doubt that these primates can acquire and use and transmit a gestural code. They may also make simple metaphors or creative couplings of signs (this has been observed in many chimps, including Washoe and Nim Chimsky). But does this, properly speaking, constitute a language? In terms of syntactic competence and generative grammar, it seems doubtful if chimpanzees can be said to have genuine language capacity. (Although Savage-Rumbaugh feels there may be a proto-grammar; see Savage-Rumbaugh, 1986).

37. (See Chomsky, 1968, p. 26.) The intellectual history of such a generative, or "philosophical" grammar, and of the concept of "innate ideas" in general, has been fascinatingly discussed by Chomsky—one feels that he needed to discover his own precursors in order to dis-

cover himself, his own place in an intellectual tradition; see especially his *Cartesian Linguistics* and his Beckman lectures, published as *Language and Mind.* The great era of "philosophical grammar" was in the seventeenth century, and its high point was the Port-Royal *Grammar* in 1660. Our present linguistics, Chomsky feels, might have arisen then, but its development was aborted by the rise of a shallow empiricism. If the notion of an underlying native propensity is extended from language to thought in general, then the doctrine of "innate ideas" (that is, structures of mind which, when activated, organize the form of experience) may be traced back to Plato, thence to Leibniz and Kant. Some biologists have felt this concept of innateness essential to explain the forms of organic life, most notably the ethologist Konrad Lorenz, whom Chomsky quotes in this context (Chomsky, 1968, p. 81):

> Adaptation of the a priori to the real world has no more originated from "experience" than adaptation of the fin of the fish to the properties of water. Just as the form of the fin is given a priori, prior to any individual negotiation of the young fish with the water, and just as it is this form that makes possible this negotiation, so it is also the case with our forms of perception and categories in their relationship to our negotiation with the real external world through experience.

Others see experience not merely as kindling but as *creating* the forms of perception and categories.

38. Chomsky, 1968, p. 76.

39. The notion of a "critical age" for acquiring language was introduced by Lenneberg: the hypothesis that if language were not acquired by puberty it would never be acquired thereafter, at least not with real, native-like proficiency. Questions of critical age hardly arise with the hearing population, for virtually all the hearing (even the retarded) acquire competent speech in the first five years of life. It is a major problem for the deaf, who may be unable to hear, or at least make any sense out of, their parents' voices, and who may also be denied any exposure to Sign. There is evidence, indeed, that those who learn Sign late (that is, after the age of five) never acquire the effort-

less fluency and flawless grammar of those who learn it from the start (especially those who acquire it earliest, from their deaf parents).

There may be exceptions to this, but they *are* exceptions. It may be accepted, in general, that the preschool years are crucial for the acquisition of good language, and that indeed, first exposure to language should come as early as possible—and that those born deaf should go to nursery schools where Sign is taught. It might be said that Massieu, at the age of thirteen and nine months, was still within this critical age, but clearly Ildefonso was far beyond this. Their very late acquisition of language could be explained simply by an unusual retention of neuronal plasticity; but a more interesting hypothesis is that the gestural systems (or "home signs") set up by Ildefonso and his brother, or by Massieu and his deaf siblings, could have functioned as a "proto-language," inaugurating, so to speak, a linguistic competence in the brain, which was only fired to full activity with exposure to genuine sign language many years later. (Itard, the physician-teacher of Victor, the Wild Boy, also postulated a critical period for language acquisition in order to explain his failure to teach Victor speech production and perception.)

40. See Corina, 1989.

41. See Lévy-Bruhl, 1966.

42. Since most research on Sign at present takes place in the United States, most of the findings relate to American Sign Language, although others (Danish, Chinese, Russian, British) are also being investigated. But there is no reason to suppose these are peculiar to ASL—they probably apply to the entire class of visuospatial languages.

43. As one learns Sign, or as the eye becomes attuned to it, it is seen to be fundamentally different in character from gesture, and is no longer to be confused with it for a moment. I found the distinction particularly striking on a recent visit to Italy, for Italian gesture (as everyone knows) is large and exuberant and operatic, whereas Italian Sign is strictly constrained within a conventional signing space, and strictly constrained by all the lexical and grammatical rules of a signed lan-

guage, and not in the least "Italianate" in quality: the difference between the para-language of gesture and the actual language of Sign is evident here, instantly, to the untutored eye.

44. See Liddell and Johnson, 1989, and Liddell and Johnson, 1986.

45. Stokoe, 1979.

46. Again, Stokoe describes some of this complexity:

When three or four signers are standing in a natural arrangement for sign conversation . . . the space transforms are by no means 180-degree rotations of the three-dimensional visual world but involve orientations that non-signers seldom if ever understand. When all the transforms of this and other kinds are made between the signer's visual three-dimensional field and that of each watcher, the signer has transmitted the content of his or her world of thought to the watcher. If all the trajectories of all the sign actions—direction and direction-change of all upper arms, forearm, wrist, hand and finger movement, all the nuances of all the eye and face and head action—could be described, we would have a description of the phenomena into which thought is transformed by a sign language. . . . These superimpositions of semantics onto the space-time manifold need to be separated out if we are to understand how language and thought and the body interact.

47. "We currently analyze three dimensional movement using a modified Op-Eye system, a monitoring apparatus permitting rapid high-resolution digitalization of hand and arm movements. . . . Opto-electronic cameras track the positions of light-emitting diodes attached to the hands and arms and provide a digital output directly to a computer, which calculates three-dimensional trajectories" (Poizner, Klima, and Bellugi, 1987, p. 27). See fig. 2.

48. Though unconscious, learning language is a prodigious task—but despite the differences in modality, the acquisition of ASL by deaf children bears remarkable similarities to the acquisition of spoken language by a hearing child. Specifically, the acquisition of grammar

seems identical, and this occurs relatively suddenly, as a reorganization, a discontinuity in thought and development, as the child moves from gesture to language, from prelinguistic pointing or gesture to a fully grammaticized linguistic system: this occurs at the same age (roughly twenty-one to twenty-four months) and in the same way, whether the child is speaking or signing.

49. It has been shown by Elissa Newport and Ted Supalla (see Rymer, 1988) that late learners of Sign—which means anyone who learns Sign after the age of five—though competent enough, never master its full subtleties and intricacies, are not able to "see" some of its grammatical complexities. It is as if the development of special linguistic-spatial ability, of a special left hemisphere function, is only fully possible in the first years of life. This is also true for speech. It is true for language in general. If Sign is not acquired in the first five years of life, but is acquired later, it never has the fluency and grammatical correctness of native Sign: some essential grammatical aptitude has been lost. Conversely, if a young child is exposed to less-than-perfect Sign (because the parents, for example, only learned Sign late), the child will nonetheless develop grammatically correct Sign—another piece of evidence for an innate grammatical aptitude in childhood.

50. The prescient Hughlings-Jackson wrote a century ago: "No doubt, by disease of some part of the brain the deaf-mute might lose his natural system of signs which are of some speech-value to him," and thought this would have to affect the left hemisphere.

51. The kinship of speech aphasia and sign aphasia is illustrated in a recent case reported by Damasio et al. in which a Wada test (an injection of sodium amytal into the left carotid artery—to determine whether or not the left hemisphere was dominant) given to a young, hearing Sign interpreter with epilepsy brought about a temporary aphasia of both speech and Sign. Her ability to speak English started to recover after four minutes; the sign aphasia lasted a minute or so longer. Serial PET scans were done throughout the procedure and showed that roughly similar portions of the left hemisphere were involved in speech and signing, although the latter seemed to require larger brain areas, in particular the left parietal lobe, as well.

52. There is considerable evidence that signing may be useful with some autistic children who are unable or unwilling to speak; Sign may allow such children a degree of communication which had seemed unimaginable (Bonvillian and Nelson, 1976). This may be in part, so Rapin feels, because some autistic children may have specific neurological difficulties in the auditory sphere, but much greater intactness in the visual sphere.

Though Sign cannot be of help with the aphasic, it *may* help the retarded and senile with very limited or eroded capacities for spoken language. This may be due in part to the graphic and iconic expressiveness of Sign, and in part to the relative motor simplicity of its movements, compared with the extreme complexity and vulnerability of the mechanism for speech.

53. There may be other ways of establishing such a formal space, as well as a great enhancement of visual-cognitive function generally. Thus with the spread of personal computers in the past decade, it has become possible to organize and move logical information in (computer) "space," to make (and rotate, or otherwise transform) the most complex three-dimensional models or figures. This has led to the development of a new sort of expertise—a power of visual imagery (especially imagery of topological transforms) and visual-logical thinking which was, in the precomputer age, distinctly rare. Virtually anyone can become a visual "adept" in this way—at least, anyone under the age of fourteen. It is much more difficult to achieve visual-computational fluency after this age, as it is much more difficult to achieve fluent language. Parents find again and again that their children can become computer whizzes where they cannot—another example, perhaps, of "critical age." It seems probable that such enhancements of visual-cognitive and visual-logical functions requires an early shift to a left hemisphere predominance.

54. Novel—yet potentially universal. For as in Martha's Vineyard, entire populations, hearing and deaf alike, can become fluent native signers. Thus the capacity—the neuronal apparatus—to acquire spatial language (and all the nonlinguistic spatial capacities that go with this) is clearly present, potentially, in everyone.

There must be countless neuronal potentials that we are born with which can develop or deteriorate according to demand. The development of the nervous system, and especially of the cerebral cortex is, within its genetic constraints, guided and molded, *sculpted*, by early experience. Thus the capacity to discriminate phonemes has a huge range in the first six months of life, but then becomes restricted by the actual speech to which infants are exposed, so that Japanese infants become unable, for example, to discriminate anymore between an "l" or an "r," and American infants, similarly, between various Japanese phonemes. Nor are we short on neurons; there is no danger that developing one potential will "use up" a limited supply of neurons and prevent the development of other potentials. There is every reason to have the richest possible environment, linguistically as well as in every other way, during the critical early period of brain plasticity and growth.

55. This linguistic use of the face is peculiar to signers, is quite different from the normal, affective use of the face, and, indeed, has a different neural basis. This has been shown very recently in experimental studies by David Corina. Pictures of faces, with expressions that could be interpreted as "affective" or "linguistic" were presented, tachistoscopically, to the right and left visual fields of deaf and hearing subjects. Hearing subjects, it was apparent, processed these in the right hemisphere, but deaf subjects showed predominance of the left hemisphere in "decoding" linguistic facial expressions.

The few cases studied of the effects of brain lesions in deaf signers upon facial recognition show a similar dissociation between the perception of affective and linguistic facial expressions. Thus, with left hemisphere lesions in signing subjects, the linguistic "propositions" of the face may become unintelligible (as part and parcel of an overall Sign aphasia), but its expressiveness, in the ordinary sense, is fully preserved. With right hemisphere lesions, conversely, there may be an inability to recognize faces or their ordinary expressions (a so-called prosopagnosia), even though they are still perceived as "propositionizing," fluently, in Sign.

This dissociation between affective and linguistic facial expressions may also extend to their production: thus one patient with a right hemisphere lesion studied by Bellugi's group was able to produce linguistic facial expressions where required, but lacked ordinary affective facial expressions.

56. The ancient insight that the loss of hearing may cause a "compensation" of sight cannot be ascribed simply to the use of Sign. All deaf—even the postlingually deaf, who stay in the world of speech—achieve some heightening of visual sensibility, and a move toward a more visual orientation in the world, as David Wright describes:

> I do not notice more but notice differently. What I do notice, and notice acutely because I have to, because for me it makes up almost the whole of the data necessary for the interpretation and diagnosis of events, is movement where objects are concerned; and in the case of animals and human beings, stance, expression, walk, and gesture. . . . For example, as somebody waiting impatiently for a friend to finish a telephone conversation with another knows when it is about to end by the words said and the intonation of the voice, so does a deaf man—like a person queuing outside a glass-panelled call-box—judge the moment when the good-byes are being said or the intention formed to replace the receiver. He notices a shift of the hand cradling the instrument, a change of stance, the head drawing a fraction of a millimetre from the earphone, a slight shuffling of the feet, and that alteration of expression which signals a decision taken. Cut off from auditory clues he learns to read the faintest visual evidence.

A similar acuity may also occur, and persist, in the hearing children of deaf parents. Thus in the case described by Arlow:

> The patient would look intently at his parents' faces from early childhood on. . . . [He] became extremely sensitive to intentions and meanings which can be communicated through expressions on the face. . . . Like his [deaf] father, he was particularly sensitive to people's faces and could make good judgements about the intentions and sincerity of those with whom he was engaged in business . . . [he] felt that in ordinary business negotiations he had a serious advantage over his opposite numbers.

57. It should not be supposed that all visual-cognitive processing in deaf signers is transferred to the left hemisphere. The disturbing (even devastating) effects of right hemisphere lesions on signing make it clear that this hemisphere is equally crucial for some of the visual-cognitive abilities underlying the capacity to sign. S. M. Kosslyn has

recently suggested that the left hemisphere may be better at image generation, and the right hemisphere at image manipulation and transformation; if this is so, lesions in opposite hemispheres may differentially affect various components of the mental imagery, and mental representation of space, in Sign. Bellugi and Neville are planning further studies to see if such differential effects (both in simple perceptual tasks and in complex forms of imagery) may indeed be found in signers with damage to one or the other hemisphere.

58. Although Neville, thus far, has obtained only electrophysiological evidence for such reallocation (neuro-imaging, PET scan studies, are planned) striking *anatomical* evidence for this has recently been obtained. Thus if newborn ferrets are centrally deafened (by cutting fibers to the chief auditory nuclei), many normally auditory pathways and centers are modified, and become exclusively visual in morphology and function (Sur et al., 1988).

59. Lenneberg, commenting on the critical age period for language acquisition (which he sees as related to the establishment of hemisphere dominance), speaks of normal lateralization being established in the congenitally deaf provided they acquire language by the age of seven. Sometimes, however, cerebral lateralization is not well established: perhaps, writes Lenneberg, "a relatively large percentage of the congenitally [and linguistically incompetent] deaf falls into this category."

Early language acquisition, whether speech or Sign, seems to kindle the linguistic powers of the left hemisphere; and deprivation of language, partial or absolute, seems to retard development and growth in the left hemisphere.

60. Cudworth writes, in the seventeenth century, of how a

skilful and expert limner will observe many elegancies and curiosities of art, and be highly pleased with several strokes and shadows in a picture, where a common eye can discern nothing at all; and a musical artist hearing a consort of exact musicians playing some excellent composure of many parts, will be exceedingly ravished with many harmonical airs and touches, that a vulgar ear will be utterly insensible of (R. Cudworth, "Treatise

Containing Eternal and Immutable Morality," cited in Chomsky, 1966).

The capacity to move from a "common eye" or "vulgar ear" into artistic skill and expertise goes with the move from right to left hemisphere predominance. There is good evidence (both from studying the effects of cerebral lesions, as A. R. Luria has done, as well as experimentally, with dichotic listening) that while musical perception is chiefly a right hemisphere function in predominantly "naive" listeners, it becomes a left hemisphere function in professional musicians and "expert" listeners (who grasp its "grammar" and rules, and for whom it has become an intricate formal structure). A special sort of "expert listening" is required for those who use Cantonese or Thai, the morphology of which relies on tonal discrimination in a way European languages do not. There is evidence that this (normally a right hemisphere function) becomes a left hemisphere function in fluent Thai speakers: it is much improved in right ear (and thus left hemisphere) listening with them, and is grossly impaired with left hemisphere strokes.

A similar shift occurs with those who become mathematical or arithmetical "experts," who become able to see mathematical concepts, or numbers, as part of a vast, well-organized universe or scheme. This may be equally true of painters and interior designers, who see space, and visual relationships, as no "common eye" can do. And it is true of those who acquire skill at whist, or Morse code, or chess. All the higher reaches of scientific or artistic intelligence, as well as banal game-playing skills, require representational systems that are functionally similar to language and develop like it; all of them seem to move into becoming left hemisphere skills.

61. There is a considerable and somewhat controversial literature on the character of cognitive function in the deaf—whether there is, in fact, a "deaf mind." There is some evidence that their strong visuality disposes deaf people to specifically "visual" (or logico-spatial) forms of memory and thinking; that, given complex problems with many stages, the deaf tend to arrange these, and their hypotheses, in logical space, whereas the hearing arrange them in a temporal (or "auditory") order (see, for example, Belmont, Karchmer, and Bourg, 1983).

Clearly, in a cultural sense, we may speak of the deaf mind, as we may speak of the Jewish or Japanese mind, a mentality distinguished by particular cultural sensibilities, images, perspectives, beliefs. But there is no neurological sense in which we can usefully speak of a Jewish or Japanese mind—whereas there may be, in relation to the deaf mind. There is an unusual number of deaf engineers, deaf architects, and deaf mathematicians, who have, among other things, great facility in picturing and thinking in three-dimensional space, picturing spatial transforms, and conceiving complex topological and abstract spaces. Probably this is partly based on a neurological disposition, on the neuropsychological or cognitive structure of the deaf mind.

Hearing children of deaf parents, who acquire Sign as a first language, and show striking visual enhancements even though they are hearing, may be not only bilingual, but "bimental," in the sense of having access to, or use of, two quite distinct modes of mental functioning. Certainly some of them will speak of "switching" not only language, but mode of thought, depending on whether they find themselves, or wish to be, in a visual (Sign) or speaking mode. And some, like Deborah H., will switch from one to the other in response to their own thinking needs. It would be of great interest to investigate this further, to find, for example, whether such "switching" corresponds to clear-cut neurophysiological transitions in the brain, from a predominantly auditory to a visual mode, and vice versa.

62. Poizner, Klima, and Bellugi, 1987, p. 206.

63. This dichotomy is reminiscent of Bruner's division into "narrative" and "paradigmatic," which he sees as the two natural, elemental modes of thought (see Bruner, 1986). One is tempted to see the narrative mode as a right hemisphere function, the paradigmatic as a left hemisphere one. In the retarded, certainly, the narrative mode of thought and language may be remarkably developed, with the paradigmatic remaining grossly defective. (See Sacks, 1985.)

64. This seemed to be the case with Genie's language, which was poor in syntax but relatively rich in vocabulary:

Genie's language resembles right-hemisphere language. The dichotic listening tests indicate that her language *is* right-hemisphere language. Thus, Genie's case may indicate that after the "critical period," the left hemisphere can no longer assume control in language acquisition, and the right hemisphere will function and predominate in the acquisition and representation of language (Curtiss, 1977, p. 216).

65. See Schlesinger, 1987.

66. There has recently been an educational experiment in Prince George's County, Maryland, with the introduction of Sign into first grade and preschool education among normal, hearing children. The children acquire it readily and enjoy it, and as they do they show significant improvement of reading and other skills. It may be that this facilitation of reading, of the ability to recognize the forms of words and letters, goes with the enhancement of spatial-analytic ability that occurs with the learning of Sign.

Even when (hearing) adults learn Sign, they too may become conscious of changes in themselves—a disposition to more vivid visual description, enhancements of visual imagery and memory, and often a freer and more direct expressive use of the body. It would be interesting to find out if there occurs to some degree, in such adults, an enhancement of visual evoked potentials such as Neville finds in hearing native signers.

Interestingly, there is *not* a good correlation between ability to learn spoken languages and ability to learn Sign. Some polyglots are taken aback at finding how "hard" it is; and other people, who have never been able to learn another spoken language, may be startled to find how "easy" Sign is. These differences may reflect differing visual powers of individuals, and have little to do with intellectual powers, or linguistic powers, in general. In adult life, basic visual powers may be capable of only limited enhancement, whereas early training, seemingly, can enhance visual powers in us all.

67. Newport and Supalla's research is discussed in Rymer, 1988.

68. Supalla, in press.

69. It should be made clear that no sign language can be considered as "primitive" compared to any other sign language (just as no extant

spoken language is more "primitive" than any other). But it is sometimes felt in the United States that ASL is by far the best sign language in the world—the best organized, the richest, the most
expressive, etc.—an attitude which has led to a certain amount of ASL
"imperialism" (causing other native sign languages, in smaller countries, to defer to, and even be replaced by, ASL). But this is a hierarchic
concept. In fact, all languages, whether signed or spoken, no matter
how new, or how limited their geographic distribution, have the same
potentials, the same range of possibility—none can be dismissed as
"primitive" or "defective." Thus British Sign Language is fully the
equal of ASL; Irish Sign Language is fully the equal of both; and so
too is Icelandic Sign Language (even though there are only seventy
deaf people in Iceland).

70. The hundreds of sign languages that have arisen spontaneously all
over the world are as distinct and strongly differentiated as the
world's range of spoken languages. There is no one universal sign language. And yet there may be universals *in* signed languages, which
help to make it possible for their users to understand one another far
more quickly than users of unrelated spoken languages could understand each other. Thus a monolingual Japanese would be lost in
Arkansas, as a monolingual American would be lost in rural Japan.
But a deaf American can make contact relatively swiftly with his signing brothers in Japan, Russia, or Peru—he would hardly be lost at all.
Signers (especially native signers) are adept at picking up, or at least
understanding, other signed languages, in a way which one would
never find among speakers (except, perhaps, in the most gifted). Some
understanding will usually be established within minutes, accomplished mostly be gesture and mime (in which signers are extraordinarily proficient). By the end of a day, a grammarless pidgin will be
established. And within three weeks, perhaps, the signer will possess a
very reasonable knowledge of the other sign language, enough to
allow detailed discussion on quite complex issues. There was an
impressive example of this in August 1988, when the National Theater of the Deaf visited Tokyo, and joined the Japan Theater of the
Deaf in a joint production. "The deaf actors in the American and
Japanese acting companies were soon chatting," reported David E.
Sanger in *The New York Times* (August 29, 1988), "and by late after-

noon during one recent rehearsal it became clear they were already on each other's wavelengths."

71. Edelman, 1987.

72. This point is made by Francis Crick in a recent article on neural networks (Crick, 1989). Crick describes a computational model, NET-talk, which, given an English text it has never seen before, babbles at first, having only random connections, but soon *learns* to pronounce words with 90 percent accuracy; thus, Crick observes, "it has learned the rules of English pronunciation, which are notoriously not straightforward, in a tacit manner, from examples only, and not because the rules have been explicitly embodied in some program." What might seem to be a "Chomskian" task, albeit a trivial one compared to the achievement of grammar, is here accomplished by a mere network of artificial neurons with initially random connections. There has been great excitement recently about such neural networks, but the actual mechanisms evolved by the brain, Crick feels, are quite unknown to us at this point, and liable to be of an altogether different (and more "biological") order and nature.

Addendum 1990: Such a network has very recently been devised (by B. P. Yuhas) to read lips, by estimating vowels based on mouth shape, and positions of lips, teeth, and tongue. This neural network, combined with conventional speech recognition systems, may one day produce a system which is fast enough and flexible enough for practical use (*Science* 247:1414, March 23, 1990).

73. It will be evident that I have moved around somewhat between a "nativist" (a Chomskian) and an "evolutionist" (an Edelmanian) viewpoint. I must confess to being emotionally attracted to a Chomskian, or Cartesian, or Platonic idealism, to the notion of our language capacities, our powers of intellectual apprehension, all our perceptual powers, being innate—and, in the most general terms, to the notion of Design; but my observations of language acquisition, and of all developments in the individual or the species, tell me a much untidier story, tell me that nothing in nature (or animate nature) is "designed" in advance, and that everything evolves, or emerges, under the pressures of contingency and selection. Thus my general movement, as I have been writing, is from a

nativist towards an evolutionist standpoint. Yet the study of Sign, and its acquisition in childhood, fascinatingly, seems to give strong support to *both* points of view, and perhaps the two are not incompatible.

74. The experiment of King Psammetichos, a seventh-century B.C. Egyptian ruler, was described by Herodotus. Other monarchs, including Charles IV of France, James IV of Scotland, and the notorious Akbar Khan, have repeated the experiment. Ironically, in the case of Akbar Khan, the infants were given over, not to shepherds who were forbidden to speak, but to deaf nurses who did not speak (but who, unknown to Akbar, signed). When, at the age of twelve, these children were brought to Akbar's court, none of them (it is true) spoke, but all of them signed. There was, it was clear, no inborn or "Adamic" language, and if no language was used, no language was acquired; but if *any* language was used, even a signed language, this would become the language of the children.

75. Schein, 1984, p. 131. Shanny Mow, in a brief autobiography excerpted by Leo Jacobs, describes this all-too-typical estrangement of a deaf child in his own home:

> You are left out of the dinner table conversation. It is called mental isolation. While everyone else is talking and laughing, you are as far away as a lone Arab on a desert that stretches along every horizon. . . . You thirst for connection. You suffocate inside but you cannot tell anyone of this horrible feeling. You do not know how to. You get the impression nobody understands or cares. . . . You are not granted even the illusion of participation. . . .
>
> You are expected to spend fifteen years in the straitjacket of speech training and lipreading . . . your parents never bother to put in an hour a day to learn sign language or some part of it. One hour of twenty-four that can change a life time for you (Jacobs, 1974, pp. 173–174).

The *only* deaf children not liable to suffer such cruel estrangements even in their own households are those who are born of deaf (and signing) parents—such children are (in the words of a deaf friend with hearing parents) "another species." Deaf children of deaf parents can enjoy, from the start, a full communication and relation with their parents; they acquire fluent language as easily and automatically as hearing children do, and at the same crucial time (in the third year of life): their Sign has a precision and a richness no non-native signer can acquire. They are more likely, very early, to meet other deaf adults and deaf children, to enter fully into an understanding community. They grow up with a firm sense of confidence, and of personal and cultural identity—their lives have been organized, from the start, around "a different center" (Padden and Humphries, 1988). Many of the "elite" in the Deaf world are born of deaf parents, and sometimes, indeed, come from large, multi-generational deaf families—this was the case with all four student leaders of the Gallaudet revolt.

A different, and unique, position is occupied by the hearing children of deaf parents, who grow up with both Sign and speech as native languages, and may be equally at ease in both deaf and hearing worlds. They often become interpreters, and they are ideally suited for this, because they can interpret not only the language, but the culture, of one world to another.

76. Hearing parents of deaf children face especially delicate and anguished issues of belonging and identity. Thus one such mother, writing to me of her own child who had been deafened at the age of five months by meningitis, wrote: "Does this mean that overnight he has suddenly become a stranger to us, that somehow he no longer *belongs* to us but to the deaf world? That he is now part of the deaf community, that we have no claim on him?" This fear that their deaf child will become estranged from them, will be taken away from them by the deaf community, is one which a good many parents of deaf children express; and it is a fear which may move them to bind the child to themselves, and to deny him access, while he is young, to Sign and other deaf people. "While his care and nurture is in *our* hands," continues my correspondent, "I feel he needs access to *our* language, in the same way as he has access to *our* food, *our* foibles, *our* family history."

There are two related issues here. One has to do with parents being able to "let go" of their children: all parents must do this, but it may need to be done at an earlier age, in some ways, with a deaf child, so that he may start on his own, so-special development. The other issue has to do with the deaf community. A deaf child does not need to be "protected" from the deaf community; the deaf community is not lying in wait to steal him from his parents. On the contrary, the deaf community is the greatest resource there is for a deaf child, and one which can be (with the parents' cooperation) a liberating force, allowing the child to acquire language and develop in his own way. It requires a special generosity of spirit for parents to realize this—for them to perceive their deaf child as he is, to unshackle him from their own wishes and needs, and to allow him to develop as a free and independent—though different—being. The deaf child needs a *double* identity. Allowing this allows mutual respect and love, whereas forbidding it is all too likely to lead to the estrangement of which Schein and Mow speak.

77. We can, of course, only guess at the origins of language—speech or Sign—or make hypotheses or inferences which cannot be directly proved or disproved. Speculation in the nineteenth century reached such peak proportions that the Paris Société de Linguistique, in 1866, finally banned the presentation of any further papers on the subject; but paleolinguistics has become a science, and there is much evidence now that was not available a century ago—evidence which points to the prehistorical origin of language in signs. This, indeed, is the title of Stokoe's 1974 paper, "Motor Signs as the First Form of Language" (see also Hewes, 1974).

There are intriguing direct observations of gestural communication between (hearing) mothers and infants prior to speech (see Tronick, Brazelton, and Als, 1978)—and if ontogeny does recapitulate phylogeny, this provides a further suggestion that the earliest human language was gestural or motor.

78. Lévy-Bruhl, describing the mentality of "primitives" (the term "primitive" for him implies earlier or more primordial, never inferior or childish), speaks of "collective representations" as central in their language, orientation, and perception. These are quite different from abstract concepts—they are "more complex states in which emotional or motor elements are *integral parts* of the representation." He speaks similarly of "image-concepts," which are both undecomposed and undecomposable. Such image-concepts are intensely visuospatial, tending to describe "the shape and contour, positions, movement, way of acting, of objects in space—in a word, all that can be perceived and delineated." Lévy-Bruhl describes the widespread development of

sign language in the hearing—sign languages that are parallel to spoken languages, and essentially identical in structure: "the two languages, the signs of which differ so widely as gestures and articulate sounds, are affiliated by their structure and their method of interpreting objects, actions, conditions. . . . Both have at their disposal a great number of fully formed visual-motor associations . . . which are called up in the mind the moment they are described." Lévy-Bruhl speaks here of "manual concepts"—"movements of the hands in which language and thought are inseparably united."

By the same token, when there is, as Lévy-Bruhl puts it, a "transition to higher mental types," this absolutely concrete language has to give way, its sensorially particular, vivid, precise "image-concepts" being replaced by imageless (and, in a sense, flavorless) logical-abstract-general concepts. (It was similarly, Sicard tells us, necessary for Massieu to abandon his metaphors and turn to more abstract, generalized adjectives.)

Vygotsky and Luria, in their youth, were deeply influenced by Lévy-Bruhl and provide similar (but more exactly studied) examples of such a transition as "primitive" agricultural cultures were "socialized" and "sovietized" in the 1920s:

> This [concrete] mode of thought . . . undergoes a radical transformation once the conditions of people's lives change. . . . Words become the principal agents of abstraction and generalization. At this point people dispense with graphic thinking and codify ideas primarily through conceptual schemes . . . they overcome, in the course of time, their inclination to think in visual terms (Luria, 1976).

One cannot avoid a certain feeling of discomfort reading descriptions such as those of Lévy-Bruhl and the young Luria—descriptions that portray the concrete as "primitive," as something to be replaced in the ascent to the abstract (this indeed has been a very general tendency in neurology and psychology for the past century). There should not be any sense of the concrete and the abstract as mutually exclusive, of the one being abandoned as one progresses to the other. On the contrary, it is precisely the richness of the concrete that gives power to the abstract. This is clearer if one is careful about defining it, and defines it in terms of "superordinate" and "subordinate."

This proper (as distinct from conventional) sense of "abstraction" is central to Vygotsky's vision of language and mind, his seeing their progress as the ability to impose superordinate structures that take in more and more of the subordinate, the concrete, by virtue of their inclusiveness, their broader perspective.

> The new higher concepts [in turn] transform the meaning of the lower. . . . The child does not have to restructure all his earlier concepts . . . once a new structure has been incorporated into his thinking . . . it gradually spreads to the older concepts as they are drawn into the intellectual operations of the higher type.

A similar image is used by Einstein, with regard to theorizing: "Creating a new theory is not like destroying an old barn and erecting a skyscraper in its place. It is rather like climbing a mountain, and gaining new and wider views."

In abstracting, or generalizing, or theorizing, as thus understood, the concrete is never lost—quite the reverse. As it is seen from a broader and broader viewpoint, so it is seen to have ever-richer and unexpected connections; it holds together, it makes sense, as never before. As one gains in generality, so one gains in concreteness; thus the vision of the older Luria that science is "the ascent to the concrete."

The beauty of language, and of Sign in particular, is like the beauty of theory in this way: that the concrete leads to the general, but it is through the general that one recaptures the concrete, intensified, transfigured. This regaining and renewal of the concrete, through the power of abstraction, is radiantly visible in a partly iconic language like Sign.

Part III: The Revolution of the Deaf

1. One can be very close to (if not actually a member of) the deaf community without being deaf. The most important prerequisite besides a knowledge of and sympathy for deaf people is being a fluent user of Sign: perhaps the only hearing people who are ever considered full members of the deaf community are the hearing children of deaf parents for whom Sign is a native language. This is the case with Dr. Henry Klopping, the much-loved superintendent of the California

School for the Deaf in Fremont. One of his former students, talking to me at Gallaudet, signed, "He is Deaf, even though he is hearing."

2. Different social conventions arise in the intercourse of signers, dictated in the first place by the differences of eye and ear. For vision is more specific than hearing—one can move one's eyes, one can focus them, one can (literally or metaphorically) shut them, whereas one cannot move or focus or shut one's ears. And signing, so to speak, is lasered in a narrow beam, to and fro, between signers, and does not diffuse in all directions, acoustically, like speaking. Thus one can have a dozen different people signing at a table, in six different conversations, each conversation clear and distinct, none of them necessarily disturbing the others. There is no "noise," no visual noise, in a room full of signers, because of the directionality of visual voices and of visual attention. By the same token (this was very clear at the huge student bar at Gallaudet, and I have seen it at large deaf banquets and conventions) one can easily sign to somebody at the other end of a large, crowded room; whereas yelling would be horrible and offensive.

There are many other (some, to the hearing, rather strange) points of Sign etiquette. One must be very conscious of eye-lines and visual contact; and avoid inadvertently walking between people and interrupting this contact. One is free to tap on shoulders and to point—not done in hearing circles. And if one finds oneself overlooking a room full of signers, with three hundred Sign conversations clearly in view, one makes a point of not "overseeing" or eavesdropping, of only seeing what one is meant to see.

At NTID in Rochester, which was built in 1968 for deaf students, one can see an architectural corollary to this. The moment one enters, one can see that this is a building for visual beings—it is designed so that signing can be seen at great distances, and sometimes between floors. One would not shout from one floor to another, but it is perfectly natural to sign from one to another.

3. The deaf world, like all subcultures, is formed partly by exclusion (from the hearing world), and partly by the formation of a community and a world around a different center—its own center. To the extent that the deaf feel excluded, they may feel isolated, set apart, discriminated against. To the extent that they form a deaf world, voluntarily,

for themselves, they are at home in it, enjoy it, see it as a haven and a buffer. In this aspect the deaf world feels self-sufficient, not isolated—it has no wish to assimilate or be assimilated; on the contrary, it cherishes its own language and images, and wishes to protect them.

One aspect of this is the so-called diglossia of the deaf. Thus a group of deaf people, at Gallaudet or elsewhere, converse in Sign among themselves; but if a hearing person should enter, they at once switch to signed English (or whatever) for a time, returning to Sign as soon as he is gone. ASL is often treated as an intimate and highly personal possession, to be shielded from intrusive or foreign eyes. Barbara Kannapell has gone to far as to suggest that if we all learned Sign, this would destroy the deaf world:

> ASL has a unifying function, since deaf people are unified by their common language. But the use of ASL simultaneously separates deaf people from the hearing world. So the two functions are different perspectives on the same reality—one from inside the group which is unified, and the other from outside. The group is separated from the hearing world. This separatist function is a protection for deaf people. For example, we can talk about anything we want, right in the middle of a crowd of hearing people. They are not supposed to understand us.
>
> It is important to understand that ASL is the only thing we have that belongs to deaf people completely. It is the only thing that has grown out of the deaf group. Maybe we are afraid to share our language with hearing people. Maybe our group identity will disappear once hearing people know ASL (Kannapell, 1980, p. 112).

4. Even those teachers who sign tend, however, to use a form of signed English rather than ASL. Except in the mathematical faculty, where a majority of the teachers are deaf, only a minority of the faculty now at Gallaudet is deaf—whereas in Edward Gallaudet's day a majority were deaf. This, alas, is still the case generally with regard to the education of the deaf. There are very few deaf teachers of the deaf; and ASL, for the most part, is either not known to, or not used by, hearing teachers.

5. Over and above the general disadvantagedness of the deaf (not through their disability, but through *our* discrimination), there are all sorts of specific problems which arise from their use of a signed

language—but these are only problems to the extent that *we* make them so. It is difficult for a deaf person, for example, to get adequate medical or legal care; there are a score of signing attorneys in the United States, but almost no signing physicians at all (and, as yet, very few paramedics or nurses who sign). There are scarcely any adequate emergency facilities for the deaf. If a deaf person becomes seriously ill, it is crucial to immobilize only one arm with IVs; to immobilize both arms may render him unable to talk. Similarly, it is often not realized that to handcuff a deaf signer is equivalent to gagging him.

6. Although the deaf are sometimes supposed to *be* silent, as well as to inhabit a world of silence, this may not be the case. They can, if they wish to, yell very loudly, and may do this to arouse the attention of others. If they speak, they may speak very loudly, and with very poor modulation, since they cannot monitor their own voices by ear. Finally, they may have unconscious and often very energetic vocalizations of various sorts—accidental or inadvertent movements of the vocal apparatus, neither intended nor monitored, tending to accompany emotion, exercise, and excited communication.

7. This resentment of "paternalism" (or "mommyism") is very evident in the special edition of the students' newspaper (*The Buff and Blue*) published on March 9, in which there is a poem entitled "Dear Mom." This starts:

> *Poor mommy Bassett-Spilman*
> *How her children do rebel,*
> *If only they would listen*
> *To the story she would tell*

and continues in this vein for thirteen verses. (Spilman had appeared on television, pleading for Zinser, saying, "Trust us—she will not disappoint you.") Copies of this poem had been reproduced by the thousand—one could see them fluttering all over campus.

8. Such considerations should be taken into account in relation to the current controversies about "special" schools or "mainstreaming." Mainstreaming—educating deaf children with the nondeaf—has the advantage of introducing the deaf to others, the world-at-large (at

least, this is the supposition); but it may also introduce an isolation of its own—and serve to cut the deaf off from their own language and culture. There is much pressure, in the United States, Canada, England, and elsewhere at this time, to shut down residential and other special schools for the deaf. Sometimes this is done under the aegis of civil rights for the handicapped, giving them the right to "equal access" or to the "least restrictive" educational environment. But the deaf—at least the profoundly and prelingually deaf, whose native and communal language is Sign—are in a very special, indeed unique, category. They cannot be compared with any other group of pupils. The deaf do not regard themselves as handicapped, but as a linguistic and cultural minority, who have the need, and indeed the right, to be together, to go to school together, to learn in a language which is accessible to them, and to live in the company and community of others of their kind.

Legislation for the handicapped, with its emphasis on equal access, takes no note of these special needs and requirements; even worse, it threatens the dissolution of a unique educational system which has also been fundamental in providing linguistic and cultural continuity for the deaf. In 1989 the state of Connecticut threatened to close the American School for the Deaf, the Hartford Asylum which was founded by Clerc and Gallaudet in 1817, which was not only the founder, but has been the guardian of deaf education in the United States for 173 years. Fortunately what would have been a rash and irrevocable move was postponed at the very last moment—but similar actions continue to threaten residential schools across the country.

The deaf student population, of course, is not homogeneous: it includes many postlingually deaf pupils, who are not native signers, and who do not identify themselves with the deaf community or with Sign; pupils such as these may indeed prefer to be mainstreamed. But there will always be prelingually deaf students whose early education and enculturation will be best accomplished in residential schools, and who must have at least the option of going to such schools, and not be mainstreamed by force. But such schools, founded in the eighteenth and nineteenth centuries, may have an anachronistic, Dickensian atmosphere. They need to be preserved, one feels—but modified, made more open, made less Victorian. Thus the old via Nomentana school in Rome, modified, is now enjoying a new lease of life, not only as a school, but as a club, an arts and theater center, and a research center for the deaf—and one to which, now, some hearing pupils and their parents also come (Pinna et al., 1990).

9. There is nothing quite equivalent, in the hearing world, to the crucial role of residential deaf schools, deaf clubs, etc.; for these, above all, are places where deaf people find a home. Deaf youngsters, sadly, may feel deeply isolated, even estranged, in their own families, in hearing schools, in the hearing world; but they can find a new family, a profound sense of homecoming, when they meet other deaf people. Schein (1989) cites these words from a young deaf man:

> My sister told me about the Maryland School for the Deaf. . . . My immediate reaction was one of anger and rejection—of myself. I reluctantly accompanied her to the School one day— and at long last began to come *home*. It was literally a love experience. For the first time, I felt less like a *stranger* in a strange land and more like a member of a community.

And Kyle and Woll cite a contemporary account of Clerc's visit to a deaf school in London in 1814:

> As soon as Clerc beheld this sight [the children at dinner] his face became animated: he was as agitated as a traveller of sensibility would be on meeting all of a sudden in distant regions, a colony of his countrymen. . . . Clerc approached them. He made signs and they answered him by signs. This unexpected communication caused a most delicious sensation in them and for us was a sense of expression and sensibility that gave us the most heartfelt satisfaction.

10. There was soon a division of the ways, with blind pupils being educated separately from the "deaf and dumb" (as the congenitally deaf, with little or no speech, used to be called). Among the two thousand deaf students at Gallaudet now, there are about twenty students who are both deaf and blind (most with Usher's syndrome). These students, of course, must develop astonishing tactile sensibility and intelligence, as Helen Keller did.

11. The protagonists in this struggle, Bell and Gallaudet—both the sons of deaf mothers (but mothers with completely different attitudes to their own deafness), each passionately devoted to the deaf in his own way, were about as different as two human beings can be (see Winefield, 1987).

12. There has been one realm where sign language always continued to be used, all over the world, despite the changed habits and proscriptions of educators—in religious services for the deaf. Priests and others never forgot the souls of their deaf parishioners, learned Sign (often from them), and conducted services in Sign, right through the endless wrangles over oralism and the eclipse of Sign in secular education. De l'Epée's concern was religious in the first instance, and this concern, with its prompt perception of the "natural language" of the deaf, has remained steadfast despite secular vicissitudes for two hundred years. This religious use of Sign is discussed by Jerome Schein:

> That sign has a spiritual aspect should not surprise anyone, especially if one considers its use by silent religious orders and by priests in the education of deaf children. What must be seen to be fully appreciated, however, is its singular appropriateness for religious worship. The depth of expression that can be achieved by signing defies accurate description. The Academy Award won by Jane Wyman in 1948 for her portrayal of a deaf girl in *Johnny Belinda* undoubtedly owed much to her beautiful (and accurate) rendering of the Lord's Prayer in Ameslan.
>
> It is perhaps in the church service that the beauty of sign becomes most evident. Some churches have sign choirs. Watching the robed members sign in unison can be an awe-inspiring experience (Schein, 1984, pp. 144–145).

In October of 1989 I visited a deaf synagogue in Arleta, in Southern California, for the solemn Day of Atonement (Yom Kippur) services. More than 200 people had gathered there, some coming from hundreds of miles away. A few people spoke, but the entire service was in Sign; the rabbi, the choir, and the congregants all signed. At the reading of the Law—the Hebrew Torah is written on a scroll, and portions of this are read by different congregants—this "reading aloud" took the form of signing, a fluent translation of biblical

Hebrew into Sign. Some extra, special prayers had been added to the service. At one point, where there is a communal atonement, of the form "We have done this, we have done that; we have sinned through doing this, we have sinned through doing that . . ." an extra "sin" was added: "We have sinned through being impatient with the hearing when they failed to understand us." And an extra prayer of thanksgiving was thrown in: "Thou hast given us hands, that we might create language."

The Sign was especially astonishing; I had never before seen such large sweeping signs, or signs in unison—nor had I seen signing not in the usual sign-space used for human, social discourse, but high up, above the shoulders, towards Heaven, to God. (There was an atmosphere of great devotion, although, just in front of me, there was a middle-aged woman gossiping on the hands with her daughter, non-stop, a Sign yenta who reminded me of the murmuring and nattering of synagogues at home.)

The congregants gathered long before the service, and stayed till long after—it was an important social and cultural, as well as religious, event. Such congregations are exceedingly rare, and I could not help wondering how it would be for a deaf child to be brought up in Montana or Wyoming, without a deaf church or deaf synagogue in thousands of miles.

13. This happened not only in the United States, but throughout the world—even de l'Epée's school, when I visited it in 1990, had become rigidly "oral" (de l'Epée, I felt, was surely turning in his grave).

14. I regret that I have not had a chance to discuss this with Carol Padden and Tom Humphries, who being themselves both deaf and scientists, are in a position to see these events both from the inside and the outside; they have provided, in their chapter on "A Changing Consciousness" in *Deaf in America*, the most insightful short account of changing attitudes to the deaf, and among the deaf, in the past thirty years.

15. Stokoe, 1980, pp. 266–267.

16. But Klima and Bellugi relate how, at a 1965 conference, when Chomsky spoke of language as "a specific sound-meaning correspon-

dence," he was asked how he would consider the sign languages of the deaf (in terms of this characterization). He showed an open mind, said that he did not see why the sound part should be crucial, and rephrased his definition of language as a "signal-meaning correspondence."

17. ASL lends itself extremely well to artistic use and transformation—far more so than any form of manually coded or signed English—partly because it is an original language, and therefore a language for original creation, for thought; and partly because its iconic and spatial nature especially allows comic, dramatic, and aesthetic accentuation (the last section of Klima and Bellugi's book is especially devoted to "The Heightened Use of Language" in Sign). In ordinary discourse, however, few deaf people speak in pure ASL—most will bring in and incorporate expressions, signs, neologisms from signed English, as suits the needs of communication. Even though, in linguistic and neurological terms, ASL and signed English are wholly distinct, there is for practical purposes a continuum, from forms of signed English at one extreme, through various forms of "pidgin" signed English (PSE), to pure or "deep" ASL at the other.

18. Teachers and others are now being encouraged to speak and sign simultaneously; this method ("Sim Com"), it is hoped, can secure the advantages of both—in practice, though, it fails to do this. Speaking itself tends to be slowed down artificially, in order to allow the signs to be made, but even so, the signing suffers, tends to be poorly performed, and may in fact omit crucial signs—so much so that those for whom it is designed, the deaf, may find it unintelligible. It should be added that it is scarcely possible to sign ASL and speak simultaneously, because the languages are totally different: it is hardly more possible than speaking English and writing Chinese at the same time—indeed, it may be neurologically impossible.

19. But there has not yet been in the United States any official attempt to provide deaf children with a bilingual education—there have only been small pilot experiments (like that reported by Michael Strong in 1988). And yet, in contrast, as Robert Johnson observes, there has been a widespread and successful use of bilingual education in

Venezuela, where this is a national policy and increasing numbers of deaf adults are being recruited as aides and teachers (Johnson, personal communication). Venezuelan schools have daycare centers where deaf children and infants are sent as early as they are diagnosed, to be exposed to deaf signing adults until they are old enough to go to nursery and grade schools, where they are instructed bilingually. A similar system has been set up in Uruguay. Both of these South American programs have already achieved notable success and hold out great promise for the future—they are, unfortunately, as yet virtually unknown to American and European educators (but see Johnson, Liddell, and Erting, 1989). The only other countries with bilingual programs for the deaf are Sweden and Denmark—where the native sign languages are officially recognized as "mother tongues" of the deaf. All of these show very clearly that one can learn to read perfectly well without speaking and that "total communication" is not a necessary intermediate between oral education and bilingual education.

20. The sociolinguist James Woodward is especially concerned with this theme. This increasing sense of cultural diversity, rather than a single fixed "norm," with "deviance" to either side, goes back to a generous tradition of a century or more earlier; in particular to the viewpoint of Laurent Clerc (and this is another, even more fundamental reason why the students invoked his name, and felt that *his* was the spirit that guided the revolt).

Clerc's teachings, until his death, had the effect of widening the nineteenth-century view of "human nature," of introducing a relativistic and egalitarian sense of great natural range, not just a dichotomy of "normal" and "abnormal." We speak of our nineteenth-century forebears as rigid, moralistic, repressive, censorious, but the tone of Clerc's voice, and of those who listened to him, conveyed quite the opposite impression: that this was an age very hospitable to "the natural"—to the whole variety and range of natural proclivities—and not disposed (or at least less disposed than our own) to make moralizing or clinical judgments on what was "normal" and what was "abnormal."

This sense of the range of nature is apparent again and again in Clerc's brief *Autobiography* (which is excerpted in Lane, 1984a). "Every creature, every work of God, is admirably made. What we find fault in its kind turns to our advantage without our knowing it." Or, again, "We can only thank God for the rich diversity of his creation, and hope that in the future world the reason for it will be explained."

Clerc's concept of "God," "creation," "nature,"—humble, appreciative, mild, unresentful—is perhaps rooted in his sense of himself, and other deaf people, as different but nonetheless complete beings. It is in great contrast to the half-terrible, half-Promethean fury of Alexander Graham Bell, who constantly sees deafness as a swindle and a privation and a tragedy, and is constantly concerned with "normalizing" the deaf, "correcting" God's blunders, and, in general, "improving on" nature. Clerc argues for cultural richness, tolerance, diversity. Bell argues for technology, for genetic engineering, hearing aids, telephones. The two types are wholly opposite but both, clearly, have their parts to play in the world.

21. A massive, illustrated *Deaf Heritage: A Narrative History of Deaf America* by Jack R. Gannon was published in 1981. Harlan Lane's books, from 1976 onwards, not only presented the history of the deaf in stirring, dramatic terms, but were themselves "political" events, serving to give the deaf an intense (perhaps partly mythical) sense of their own past and an urge to regain the best of the past in the future. Thus they not only recorded history, they helped to make it as well (just as Lane himself was not just a recorder, but an active participant, in the 1988 revolt).

22. So, at least, the matter seemed to outside observers—the deaf revolting against the label of "disabled." Those within the deaf community were inclined to put it differently, to assert that they had never seen themselves as disabled. Padden and Humphries are emphatic on this point:

"Disabled" is a label that historically has not belonged to Deaf people. It suggests political self-representations and goals unfamiliar to the group. When Deaf people discuss their deafness, they use terms deeply related to their language, their past, and their community. Their enduring concerns have been the preservation of their language, policies for educating deaf children, and maintenance of their social and political organizations. The modern language of "access" and "civil rights," as unfamiliar as it is to

Deaf people, has been used by Deaf leaders because the public understands these concepts more readily than ones specific to the Deaf community (Padden and Humphries, 1988, p. 44).

23. It should not be thought that even the most avid signer is against other modes of communication when necessary. Life for deaf people has been altered immensely by various technical devices in the past twenty years, such as closed captioned TV, and teletypewriters (TTY; now TDD, or telecommunication devices for the deaf)—devices that would have delighted Alexander Graham Bell (who had originally invented the telephone, partly, as an aid for the deaf). The 1988 strike at Gallaudet could hardly have got going without such devices, which the students exploited brilliantly.

And yet TTYs have a negative side, too. Before they were widely available, fifteen years ago, deaf people went to great lengths to meet each other—they would constantly visit each other's homes, and would go regularly to their local deaf club. These were the only chances to talk with other deaf people; this constant visiting or meeting at clubs formed vital links which bound the deaf community into a close physical whole. Now, with TTYs (in Japan, faxes are used), there is much less actual visiting among the deaf; deaf clubs are starting to be deserted and empty; and a new, worrying tenuity has set in. It may be that TTYs (and closed captions or signed programs on television) give deaf people the sense of being together in an electronic village—but an electronic village is not like a real one, and the downfall of visiting and going to clubs is not readily reversed.

24. Although the choice of King Jordan delighted almost everyone, one faction saw his election as a compromise (since he was postlingually deaf), and supported instead Harvey Corson, superintendent of the Louisiana School for the Deaf, and the third finalist, who is both prelingually deaf and a native signer.

25. Though the level of political and public awareness in Europe may not yet match that in the United States, there are other ways in which the European deaf communities are more advanced. European signers are far more experienced, and far more skilled, than their American counterparts in establishing communication with deaf people from

other countries—and this is the case not only between individuals, but at meetings where people with a dozen different sign languages may come together. There is an artificial, invented system of gestures and signs called Gestuno, on the analogy of Ido or Esperanto; but the real mode of communication is increasingly the so-called International Sign Language, which draws upon the vocabularies and patterns of everyone present, and is, so to speak, continually improvised and enriched between them. ISL has been evolving, becoming richer, more formalized, more language-like for three decades—although it is still, in essence, a contact language, *a lingua franca*. It should be stressed that such "interlingual" communication between the deaf, which can develop with remarkable rapidity and sophistication—far beyond anything which can occur with speakers of different tongues—is rather mysterious, and is a subject of intense investigation at this time.

Not only do European deaf people tend to travel a great deal—for they can overcome language barriers much more easily than the hearing do—they often marry deaf people from other countries, and thus much interlingual migration takes place. It would be improbable and difficult for a Welshman, say, to settle in Finland, or vice versa; but such migrations (at least within Europe) are not all that uncommon among deaf people. For the deaf community is a supranational one, not unlike the world community of Jews, or other ethnic and cultural groups. We may, in fact, be seeing the beginnings of a pan-European deaf community—a community which may well spread beyond Europe, because the deaf community spans the entire world.

This, indeed, became very evident at a remarkable international festival and conference of deaf people, the Deaf Way, held in July 1989 in Washington, D.C. This was attended by more than 5,000 deaf people, coming from more than eighty countries across the world. As one entered the vast lobby of the conference hotel, one could see dozens of different sign languages being used; yet, by the end of a week, communication among different nationalities was relatively easy—not the Babel which would surely have resulted with dozens of spoken languages. There were eighteen national theaters of the deaf—one could, if one wished, see *Hamlet* in Italian Sign, *Oedipus* in Russian Sign, or all sorts of new Sign plays in a dozen and a half different sign languages. An International Deaf Club was formed, and one saw the beginnings, or the emergence, of a global deaf community.

REFERENCES

Arlow, J. A. 1976. "Communication and Character: A Clinical Study of a Man Raised by Deaf-Mute Parents." *The Psychoanalytic Study of the Child* 31: 139–163.

Baker, Charlotte, and Battison, Robbin, eds. 1980. *Sign Language and the Deaf Community: Essays in Honor of William C. Stokoe.* Silver Spring, Md.: National Association of the Deaf.

Bell, Alexander Graham. 1883. *Memoir Upon the Formation of a Deaf Variety of the Human Race.* New Haven: National Academy of Science.

Bellugi, Ursula. 1980. "Clues from the Similarities Between Signed and Spoken Language." In *Signed and Spoken Language: Biological Constraints on Linguistic Form,* ed. U. Bellugi and M. Studdert-Kennedy. Weinheim and Deerfield Beach, Fla.: Verlag Chemie.

Bellugi, Ursula and Newkirk, Don. 1981. "Formal Devices for Creating New Signs in American Sign Language." *Sign Language Studies* 30: 1–33.

Bellugi, U.; O'Grady, L.; Lillo-Martin, D.; O'Grady, M.; van Hoek, K.; and Corina, D. 1989. "Enhancement of Spatial Cognition in Hearing and Deaf Children." In *From Gesture to Language in Hearing Children,* ed. V. Volterra and C. Erting. New York: Springer Verlag.

Belmont, John; Karchmer, Michael; and Bourg, James W. 1983. "Structural Influences on Deaf and Hearing Children's Recall of Temporal/Spatial Incongruent Letter Strings." *Educational Psychology* 3, nos. 3–4: 259–274.

Bonvillian, J. D., and Nelson, K. E. 1976. "Sign Language Acquisition in a Mute Autistic Boy." *Journal of Speech and Hearing Disorders* 41:339–347.

Bragg, Bernard. 1989. *Lessons in Laughter* (as signed to Eugene Bergman). Washington, D.C.: Gallaudet University Press.

Brown, Roger. 1958. *Words and Things.* Glencoe, Ill.: The Free Press.

Bruner, Jerome. 1966. *Towards a Theory of Instruction.* Cambridge, Mass.: Harvard University Press.

————. 1983. *Child's Talk: Learning to Use Language.* New York and Oxford: Oxford University Press.

————. 1986. *Actual Minds, Possible Worlds.* Cambridge, Mass., and London: Harvard University Press.

Bullard, Douglas. 1986. *Islay.* Silver Spring, Md.: T. J. Publishers.

Burlingham, Dorothy. 1972. *Psychoanalytic Studies of the Sighted and the Blind.* New York: International Universities Press.

Changeux, J.-P. 1985. *Neuronal Man.* New York: Pantheon Books.

Chomsky, Noam. 1957. *Syntactic Structures.* 'S-Gravenhage: Mouton.

————. 1966. *Cartesian Linguistics.* New York: Harper & Row.

————. 1968. *Language and Mind.* New York: Harcourt, Brace and World.

Church, Joseph. 1961. *Language and the Discovery of Reality.* New York: Random House.

Conrad, R. 1979. *The Deaf Schoolchild: Language and Cognitive Function.* London and New York: Harper & Row.

Corina, David P. 1989. "Recognition of Affective and Noncanonical Linguistic Facial Expressions in Hearing and Deaf Subjects." *Brain and Cognition* 9, no. 2: 227–237.

Crick, Francis. 1989. "The Recent Excitement About Neural Networks." *Nature* 337 (January 12, 1989): 129–132.

Critchley, MacDonald. 1939. *The Language of Gesture*. London: Arnold.

Curtiss, Susan. 1977. *Genie: A Psycholinguistic Study of a Modern-Day "Wild Child."* New York: Academic Press.

Damasio, A.; Bellugi, U.; Damasio, H.; Poizner, H.; and van Gilder, J. 1986. "Sign Language Aphasia During Left-Hemisphere Amytal Injection." *Nature* 322 (July 24, 1986): 363–365.

de l'Epée, C. M. 1776. *Institution des Sourds-Muets par la voie des signes méthodiques.* Paris: Nyon. Excerpts were published in English: *American Annals of the Deaf,* 1861. 13: 8–29.

Eastman, Gilbert. 1980. "From Student to Professional: A Personal Chronicle of Sign Language." In *Sign Language and the Deaf Community,* ed. C. Baker and R. Battison. Silver Spring, Md.: National Association of the Deaf.

Edelman, Gerald M. 1987. *Neural Darwinism: The Theory of Neuronal Group Selection.* New York: Basic Books.

———. 1990. *The Remembered Present.* New York: Basic Books.

Erting, Carol J.; Prezioso, Carlene; and Hynes, Maureen O'Grady. 1989. "The Interactional Context of Deaf Mother-Infant Communication." In *From Gesture to Language in Hearing and Deaf Children,* ed. V. Volterra and C. Erting. New York: Springer Verlag.

Fant, Louie. 1980. "Drama and Poetry in Sign Language: A Personal Reminiscence." In *Sign Language and the Deaf Community,* ed. C. Baker and R. Battison. Silver Spring, Md.: National Association of the Deaf.

Fischer, Susan D. 1978. "Sign Languages and Creoles." In *Understanding Language Through Sign Language Research,* ed. Patricia Siple. New York: Academic Press.

Fraser, George R. 1976.*The Causes of Profound Deafness in Childhood.* Baltimore: Johns Hopkins University Press.

Furth, Hans G. 1966. *Thinking without Language: Psychological Implications of Deafness.* New York: Free Press.

Gallaudet, Edward Miner. 1983. *History of the College for the Deaf, 1857–1907.* Washington, D.C.: Gallaudet College Press.

Gannon, Jack R. 1981. *Deaf Heritage: A Narrative History of Deaf America.* Silver Spring, Md.: National Association of the Deaf.

Gee, James Paul, and Goodhart, Wendy. 1988. "ASL and the Biological Capacity for Language." In *Language Learning and Deafness,* ed. Michael Strong. New York and Cambridge: Cambridge University Press.

Geertz, Clifford. 1973. *The Interpretation of Cultures.* New York: Basic Books.

Goldberg, E. 1989. "The Gradiential Approach to Neocortical Functional Organization." *Journal of Clinical and Experimental Neuropsychology* 11, no. 4:489–517.

Goldberg, E., and Costa, L. D. 1981. "Hemispheric Differences in the Acquisition of Descriptive Systems." *Brain and Language* 14: 144–173.

Goldberg, E.; Vaughan, H. G.; and Gerstman, L. G. 1978. "Nonverbal Descriptive Systems and Hemispheric Asymmetry: Shape Versus Texture Discrimination." *Brain and Language* 5: 249–257.

Goldin-Meadow, S., and Feldman, H. 1977. "The Development of Language-like Communication without a Language Model." *Science* 197: 401–403.

Grant, Brian, ed. 1987. *The Quiet Ear: Deafness in Literature.* Preface by Margaret Drabble. London: Andre Deutsch.

Gregory, Richard. 1974. *Concepts and Mechanisms of Perception.* London: Duckworth.

Groce, Nora Ellen. 1985. *Everyone Here Spoke Sign Language: Hereditary Deafness on Martha's Vineyard.* Cambridge, Mass., and London: Harvard University Press.

Head, Henry, 1926. *Aphasia and Kindred Disorders of Speech.* Cambridge: Cambridge University Press.

Heffner, H. E., and Heffner, R. S. 1988. "Cortical Deafness Cannot Account for 'Sensory Aphasia' in Japanese Macaques." *Society for Neuroscience Abstracts,* 14(2): 1099.

Helmholtz, Hermann L. F. 1875. *The Sensations of Tone, as a Physiological Basis for the Theory of Music*, trans. A. J. Ellis. London: Longmans, Green & Co. (Original German edition, 1862.)

Hewes, Gordon. 1974. "Language in Early Hominids." In *Language Origins*, ed. W. Stokoe. Silver Spring, Md.: Linstok Press.

Hughlings-Jackson, John. 1915. "Hughlings-Jackson on Aphasia and Kindred Affections of Speech, together with a complete bibliography of his publications on speech and a reprint of some of the more important papers." *Brain* XXXVIII: 1–190.

Hull, John M. 1990. *Touching the Rock: An Experience of Blindness.* London: SPCK.

Hutchins, S.; Poizner, H.; McIntire, M.; Newkirk, D.; and Zimmerman, J. 1986. "A Computerized Written Form of Sign Languages as an Aid to Language Learning." In *Proceedings of the Annual Congress of the Italian Computing Society* (AICA), Palermo, Italy, 141–151.

Itard, Jean-Marc. 1932. *The Wild Boy of Aveyron*, trans. G. and M. Humphrey. New York: Century.

Jacobs, Leo M. 1974. *A Deaf Adult Speaks Out.* Washington, D.C.: Gallaudet College Press.

James, William. 1893. "Thought Before Language: A Deaf-Mute's Recollections." *American Annals of the Deaf* 38, no. 3: 135–145.

Johnson, Robert E.; Liddell, Scott K.; and Erting, Carol J. 1989. "Unlocking the Curriculum: Principles for Achieving Access in Deaf Education." Gallaudet Research Institute Working Paper 89–3.

Kisor, Henry. 1990. *What's that Pig Outdoors: A Memoir of Deafness.* New York: Hill and Wang.

Kannapell, Barbara. 1980. "Personal Awareness and Advocacy in the Deaf Community." In *Sign Language and the Deaf Community*, ed. C. Baker and R. Battison. Silver Spring, Md.: National Association of the Deaf.

Klima, Edward S., and Bellugi, Ursula. 1979. *The Signs of Language.* Cambridge, Mass.: Harvard University Press.

Knox, Jane E. 1989. "The Changing Face of Soviet Defectology: A Study in Rehabilitation of the Handicapped." *Studies in Soviet Thought* 37: 217–236.

Kosslyn, S. M. 1987. "Seeing and Imagining in the Cerebral Hemispheres: A Computational Approach." *Psychological Review* 94: 148–175.

Kuschel, R. 1973. "The Silent Inventor: The Creation of a Sign Language by the Only Deaf-mute on a Polynesian Island." *Sign Language Studies* 3: 1–27.

Kyle, J. G., and Woll, B. 1985. *Sign Language: The Study of Deaf People and Their Language.* Cambridge: Cambridge University Press.

Lane, Harlan. 1976. *The Wild Boy of Aveyron.* Cambridge, Mass.: Harvard University Press.

———. 1984a. *When the Mind Hears: A History of the Deaf.* New York: Random House.

———, ed. 1984b. *The Deaf Experience: Classics in Language and Education,* trans. Franklin Philip. Cambridge, Mass., and London: Harvard University Press.

Lenneberg, Eric H. 1967. *Biological Foundations of Language.* New York: John Wiley & Sons.

Lévy-Bruhl, Lucien. 1966. *How Natives Think.* New York: Washington Square Press. Originally published in 1910 as *Les Fonctions Mentales dans Sociétés Inférieures.*

Liddell, Scott. 1980. *American Sign Language Syntax.* The Hague: Mouton.

Liddell, Scott K., and Johnson, Robert E. 1986. "American Sign Language Compound Formation Processes, Lexicalization, and Phonological Remnants." *Natural Language and Linguistic Theory* 4: 445–513.

———. 1989. *American Sign Language: The Phonological Basis.* Silver Spring, Md.: Linstok Press. In *Sign Language Studies* 64: 195–277.

Luria, A. R. 1976. *Cognitive Development: Its Cultural and Social Foundations.* Cambridge, Mass.: Harvard University Press.

Luria, A. R. and Yudovich, F. Ia. 1958. *Speech and the Development of Mental Processes in the Child.* London: Staples Press.

Mahler, M.; Pine, F.; and Bergman, A. 1975. *The Psychological Birth of the Human Infant.* New York: Basic Books.

Mann, Edward John. 1836. *The Deaf and the Dumb.* N.p.: Hitchcock.

Miller, Jonathan. 1976. "The Call of the Wild." *New York Review of Books,* September 16.

Myklebust, Helmer R. 1960. *The Psychology of Deafness.* New York and London: Grune & Stratton.

Neisser, Arden. 1983. *The Other Side of Silence.* New York: Alfred A. Knopf.

Neville, Helen J. 1988. "Cerebral Organization for Spatial Attention." In *Spatial Cognition: Brain Bases and Development,* ed. J. Stiles-Davis, M. Kritchevsky, and U. Bellugi. Hillsdale, N.J.: Hove; and London: Lawrence J. Erlbaum.

———. 1989. "Neurobiology of Cognitive and Language Processing: Effects of Early Experience." In *Brain Maturation and Behavioral Development,* ed. K. Gibson and A. C. Petersen. Hawthorn, N.Y.: Aldine Gruyter Press.

Neville, H. J., and Bellugi, U. 1978. "Patterns of Cerebral Specialization in Congenitally Deaf Adults: A Preliminary Report." In *Understanding Language Through Sign Language Research,* ed. Patricia Siple. New York: Academic Press.

Newkirk, Don. 1987. *SignFont Handbook.* San Diego: Emerson & Stern Associates.

Padden, Carol. 1980. "The Deaf Community and the Culture of Deaf People." In *Sign Language and the Deaf Community,* ed. C. Baker and R. Battison. Silver Spring, Md.: National Association of the Deaf.

Padden, Carol, and Humphries, Tom. 1988. *Deaf in America: Voices from a Culture.* Cambridge, Mass., and London: Harvard University Press.

Penrose, Roger. 1989. *The Emperor's New Mind.* New York: Oxford University Press.

Petitto, Laura A., and Bellugi, Ursula. 1988. "Spatial Cognition and Brain Organization: Clues from the Acquisition of a Language in Space." In *Spatial Cognition: Brain Bases and Development*, ed. J. Stiles-Davis, M. Kritchevsky, and U. Bellugi. Hillsdale, N.J.: Hove; and London: Lawrence J. Erlbaum.

Pinna, P.; Rampelli, L.; Rossini, P.; and Volterra, V. 1990. "Written and Unwritten Records from a Residential School in Rome." *Sign Language Studies* 67:127–140.

Poizner, Howard; Klima, Edward S.; and Bellugi, Ursula. 1987. *What the Hands Reveal about the Brain*. Cambridge, Mass., and London: MIT Press.

Rapin, Isabelle. 1979. "Effects of Early Blindness and Deafness on Cognition." In *Congenital and Acquired Cognitive Disorders*, ed. Robert Katzman. New York: Raven Press.

———. 1986. "Helping Deaf Children Acquire Language: Lessons from the Past." *International Journal of Pediatric Otorhinolaryngology* 11: 213–223.

Restak, Richard M. 1988. *The Mind*. New York: Bantam Books.

Rymer, Russ. 1988. "Signs of Fluency." *The Sciences*, September 1988: 5–7.

Sacks, Oliver. 1985. *The Man Who Mistook His Wife for a Hat*. New York: Summit Books.

Savage-Rumbaugh, E. S. 1986. *Ape Language: From Conditioned Response to Symbol*. New York: Columbia University Press.

Schaller, Susan. 1991. *A Man without Words*. New York: Summit Books.

Schein, Jerome D. 1984. *Speaking the Language of Sign: The Art and Science of Signing*. Garden City, N.Y.: Doubleday.

———. 1989. *At Home Among Strangers*. Washington, D.C.: Gallaudet University Press.

Schlesinger, Hilde. 1987. "Dialogue in Many Worlds: Adolescents and Adults—Hearing and Deaf." In *Innovations in the Habilitation and*

Rehabilitation of Deaf Adolescents, ed. Glenn B. Anderson and Douglas Watson. Arkansas Research and Training Center.

————. 1988. "Questions and Answers in the Development of Deaf Children." In *Language Learning and Deafness*, ed. Michael Strong. Cambridge and New York: Cambridge University Press.

Schlesinger, Hilde S., and Meadow, Kathryn P. 1972. *Sound and Sign: Childhood Deafness and Mental Health*. Berkeley, Los Angeles, London: University of California Press.

Shattuck, Roger. 1987. *The Forbidden Experiment: The Story of the Wild Boy of Aveyron*. New York: Farrar, Straus & Giroux.

Shengold, Leonard. 1988. *Halo in the Sky: Observations on Anality and Defense*. New York: Guilford Press.

Stern, Daniel N. 1985. *The Interpersonal World of the Infant*. New York: Basic Books.

Stokoe, William C. 1960. *Sign Language Structure*. Reissued, Silver Spring, Md.: Linstok Press.

————. 1974. "Motor Signs as the First Form of Language." In *Language Origins*, ed. W. Stokoe. Silver Spring, Md.: Linstok Press.

————. 1979. "Syntactic Dimensionality: Language in Four Dimensions." Presented at the New York Academy of Sciences, November 1979.

————. 1980. Afterword. In *Sign Language and the Deaf Community*, ed. C. Baker and R. Battison, Silver Spring, Md.: National Association of the Deaf.

————. 1987. "Sign Writing Systems." In *Gallaudet Encyclopedia of Deaf People and Deafness*, vol. 3, ed. John Van Cleve. New York: McGraw-Hill.

Stokoe, William C.; Casterline, Dorothy C.; and Croneberg, Carl G. 1976. *A Dictionary of American Sign Language on Linguistic Principles*. Revised ed., Silver Spring, Md.: Linstok Press.

Strong, Michael. 1988. "A Bilingual Approach to the Education of Young Deaf Children: ASL and English." In *Language Learning and*

Deafness, ed. M. Strong. Cambridge and New York: Cambridge University Press.

Supalla, Samuel J. In Press. "Manually Coded English: The Modality Question in Signed Language Development." In *Theoretical Issues in Sign Language Research, vol. 2: Acquisition,* ed. Patricia Siple. Chicago: University of Chicago Press.

Supalla, Ted, and Newport, Elissa. 1978. "How Many Seats in a Chair?: The Derivation of Nouns and Verbs in American Sign Language." In *Understanding Language through Sign Language Research,* ed. Patricia Siple. New York: Academic Press.

Sur, Mriganka; Garraghty, Preston E.; and Roe, Anna W. 1988. "Experimentally Induced Visual Projections into Auditory Thalamus and Cortex," *Science* 242: 1437–1441.

Tronick, E.; Brazelton, T. B.; and Als, H. M. 1978. "The Structure of Face-to-face Interaction and Its Developmental Function." *Sign Language Studies* 18: 1–16.

Tylor, E. B. 1874. *Researches into the Early History of Mankind.* London: Murray.

Van Cleve, John V., ed. 1987. *Gallaudet Encyclopedia of Deaf People and Deafness.* New York: McGraw-Hill.

von Feuerbach, Anselm. 1834. *Caspar Hauser: An account of an individual kept in a dungeon, separated from all communication with the world, from early childhood to about the age of seventeen.* London: Simpkin & Marshall. Original German edition (1832) published as *Kaspar Hauser.*

Vygotsky, L. S. 1962. *Thought and Language,* ed. and trans. by Eugenia Hanfmann and Gertrude Vahar. Cambridge, Mass., and New York: MIT Press and John Wiley & Sons. Original Russian edition published in 1934.

Vygotsky, L. S. 1991. *The Collected Works of L. S. Vygotsky, vol. II, Problems of Abnormal Psychology and Learning Disabilities: The Fundamentals of Defectology* (Russian title: *Principles of Defectology*), ed. R. Rieber and A. S. Carton, trans. J. E. Knox and C. Stevens. New York: Plenum Press.

Walker, Lou Ann. 1986. *A Loss for Words: The Story of Deafness in a Family.* New York: Harper & Row.

Washabaugh, William. 1986. *Five Fingers for Survival.* Ann Arbor: Karoma.

Whorf, Benjamin Lee. 1956. *Language, Thought, and Reality.* Cambridge: Technology Press.

Winefield, Richard. 1987. *Never the Twain Shall Meet: Bell, Gallaudet and the Communications Debate.* Washington, D.C.: Gallaudet University Press.

Winnicott, D. W. 1965. *The Maturational Process and the Facilitating Environment.* New York: International Universities Press.

Wittgenstein, Ludwig. 1953. *Philosophical Investigations.* London: Blackwell.

Wood, David; Wood, Heather; Griffiths, Amanda; and Howarth, Ian. 1986. *Teaching and Talking with Deaf Children.* Chichester and New York: John Wiley & Sons.

Woodward, James. 1978. "Historical Bases of American Sign Language." In *Understanding Language Through Sign Language Research,* ed. Patricia Siple. New York: Academic Press.

————. 1982. *How You Gonna Get to Heaven if You Can't Talk with Jesus: On Depathologizing Deafness.* Silver Spring, Md.: T. J. Publishers.

Wright, David. 1969. *Deafness.* New York: Stein and Day. (Reprinted in 1990 by Faber and Faber, London.)

Zaidel, E. 1981. "Lexical Organization in the Right Hemisphere." In *Cerebral Correlates of Conscious Experience,* ed. P. Buser and A. Rougeul-Buser. Amsterdam: Elsevier.

SELECTED BIBLIOGRAPHY

HISTORY OF THE DEAF

The fullest history of deaf people, from their liberation in the 1750s to the (deadly) Milan conference of 1880, is given in Harlan Lane's *When the Mind Hears: A History of the Deaf.*

Excerpts from autobiographies of the first literate deaf and their teachers, during this period, are to be found in Harlan Lane, ed., *The Deaf Experience: Classics in Language and Education*, translated by Franklin Philip.

A pleasant, informal history of the deaf, full of personal vignettes and fascinating illustrations, is provided by Jack R. Gannon in *Deaf Heritage: A Narrative History of Deaf America.*

Edward Gallaudet himself wrote a half-autobiographical history of Gallaudet College, *History of the College for the Deaf, 1857–1907.*

A remarkably informative and lengthy article, under the heading of "Deaf and Dumb," may be found in the "scholars'" (11th) edition of the *Encyclopedia Britannica.*

ISLANDS OF THE DEAF

An extremely vivid, poignant account of the unique Martha's Vineyard community is Nora Ellen Groce's *Everyone Here Spoke Sign Language: Hereditary Deafness on Martha's Vineyard.*

BIOGRAPHIES AND AUTOBIOGRAPHIES

David Wright's *Deafness* is the most beautiful account of acquired deafness known to me.

A more recent book by Lou Ann Walker, *A Loss for Words: The Story of Deafness in a Family*, draws a powerful picture of life as a hearing child of deaf parents.

The Quiet Ear: Deafness in Literature, compiled by Brian Grant, with a preface by Margaret Drabble, is an extremely readable and varied anthology of short pieces by or about deaf people.

A vivid account of a rich, creative life is *Lessons in Laughter* by the eminent deaf actor Bernard Bragg. Interestingly, this was not written (though Bragg, a Shakespearean actor, is intensely literate), but *signed* (for Sign, not English, is Bragg's first language) and then translated into English.

Another fascinating account of a full and creative life is *What's that Pig Outdoors*, by the book editor of the Chicago *Sun-Times*, Henry Kisor. Kisor lost his hearing at three and a half, when he had already acquired speech and language—he does not sign, but lip-reads and speaks. Kisor does not identify himself as culturally Deaf, and his life, unlike Bernard Bragg's, has been spent entirely in the hearing world.

THE COMMUNITY AND LANGUAGE OF THE DEAF

Demographic surveys are usually dull, but Jerome Schein is incapable of being dull. *The Deaf Population of the United States*, by Jerome D. Schein and Marcus T. Delk, Jr., provides a vivid cross-section of the deaf population in the United States fifteen years ago, at a time when major changes were just starting to occur. Also recommended are Schein's *Speaking the Language of Sign* and *At Home Among Strangers*.

It is interesting to compare and contrast the situation of the deaf and their Sign in Britain. A fine account is given by J. G. Kyle and B. Woll, in *Sign Language: The Study of Deaf People and Their Language*.

A splendid overview of the deaf community is *Sign Language and the Deaf Community: Essays in Honor of William C. Stokoe*, edited by Charlotte Baker and Robbin Battison. There is not a single essay in this volume that is less than fascinating—and there is also an important and moving looking-back by Stokoe himself.

An extraordinary book—the more so because its authors are deaf, and can speak from within (as well as about) the deaf community—its organization, its aspirations, its images, its beliefs, its arts, its language, etc.—is *Deaf in America: Voices from a Culture* by Carol Padden and Tom Humphries.

Also very accessible for the general reader and full of vivid interviews with members of the deaf community is Arden Neisser's *The Other Side of Silence: Sign Language and the Deaf Community in America.*

A real treasure for browsing (even if the volumes are a little too heavy to read in bed, and a little too costly to read in the bath) is the *Gallaudet Encyclopedia of Deaf People and Deafness*, edited by John Van Cleve. One of the delights of this encyclopedia (as of all the best encyclopedias) is that one can open it anywhere and find illumination and enjoyment.

CHILD DEVELOPMENT AND EDUCATION OF THE DEAF

In the works of Jerome Bruner one can trace how a revolutionary psychology can in turn revolutionize education. Particularly remarkable in this context are Bruner's *Towards a Theory of Instruction* and his *Child's Talk: Learning to Use Language.*

An important "Bruneresque" study of the development and education of deaf children is provided by David Wood, Heather Wood, Amanda Griffiths, and Ian Howarth in *Teaching and Talking with Deaf Children.*

Hilde Schlesinger's recent work is only to be found in the professional literature, which is not always readily available. But her earlier book is both vivid and accessible: Hilde S. Schlesinger and Kathryn P. Meadow, *Sound and Sign: Childhood Deafness and Mental Health.*

Observation and psychoanalysis are powerfully combined in Dorothy Burlingham's *Psychoanalytic Studies of the Sighted and the Blind;* one wishes a similar study could be made of deaf children.

Daniel Stern also conjoins direct observation and analytic construction in *The Interpersonal World of the Infant.* Stern is particularly interesting on the development of a "verbal self."

GRAMMAR, LINGUISTICS, AND SIGN

The linguistic genius of our time is Noam Chomsky, who has written a dozen books on language since his revolutionary (1957) *Syntactic Structures*. I find the most vivid and readable are his 1967 Beckman Lectures, reprinted as *Language and Mind*.

The central figure in Sign linguistics, since 1970, has been Ursula Bellugi. None of her work is exactly popular reading, but one can glimpse fascinating vistas and dip with much pleasure into the encyclopedic *The Signs of Language* by Edward S. Klima and Ursula Bellugi. Bellugi and her colleagues have also been the foremost investigators of the neural basis of Sign; here too one may gain a sense of the fascinations of the subject in Howard Poizner, Edward S. Klima, and Ursula Bellugi, *What the Hands Reveal About the Brain*.

GENERAL BOOKS ABOUT LANGUAGE

Highly readable, witty, and provocative is Roger Brown's *Words and Things*.

Also readable, magnificent, though sometimes too dogmatic, is Eric H. Lenneberg's *Biological Foundations of Language*.

The deepest and most beautiful explorations of all are to be found in L. S. Vygotsky's *Thought and Language*, originally published in Russian, posthumously, in 1934, and later translated by Eugenia Hanfmann and Gertrude Vahar. Vygotsky has been described—not unjustly—as "the Mozart of psychology."

A personal favorite of mine is Joseph Church's *Language and the Discovery of Reality: A Developmental Psychology of Cognition*, a book one goes back to again and again.

CULTURAL ANTHROPOLOGY

Though he may (or may not) be dated, there is great interest in all the works of Lucien Lévy-Bruhl, and his incessant pondering on "primitive" language and thought: his first book, *How Natives Think*, originally published in 1910, gives the flavor of him well.

Clifford Geertz's *The Interpretation of Cultures* has to be by one's side the moment one thinks about "culture"—and it is a crucial corrective to primitive, romantic thoughts about pure and unadulterated, uncultivated human nature.

But, equally, one has to read Rousseau—to read him again in the light of the deaf and their language: I find his *Discourse on the Origin of Inequality* the richest, the most balanced, of his works.

WILD AND ISOLATED HUMAN BEINGS

Unique views of what human beings are like if deprived of their normal language and culture are provided by these rare and fearful, but crucially important human phenomena (each of which, Lord Monboddo says, is more important than the discovery of 30,000 stars). Thus, not accidentally, Harlan Lane's first book was *The Wild Boy of Aveyron*. Another superb story is Roger Shattuck's *The Forbidden Experiment: The Story of the Wild Boy of Aveyron*.

Anselm von Feuerbach's 1832 account of Kaspar Hauser is one of the most amazing psychological documents of the nineteenth century. In English, it was published as *Caspar Hauser*.

It is again more than coincidental that Werner Herzog conceived and directed not only a very powerful film of Kaspar Hauser, but also a film on the deaf and the blind, *Land of Darkness and Silence*.

The deepest contemporary pondering on "the soul murder" of Kaspar Hauser is to be found in a brilliant psychoanalytical essay by Leonard Shengold, in *Halo in the Sky: Observations on Anality and Defense*.

It is well worth looking at Susan Curtiss's minutely detailed study of a "wild child" found in California in 1970, *Genie: A Psycholinguistic Study of a Modern-Day "Wild Child."*

Finally, an enthralling and minutely-detailed account of a modern-day Massieu, a deaf man who reached adulthood with no language of any sort, but later acquired language, and how his life and mind changed with this, has been provided by Susan Schaller in *A Man without Words*.

Index